SWEET & NATURAL

SWEET & NATURAL

DESSERTS WITHOUT SUGAR, HONEY, MOLASSES OR ARTIFICIAL SWEETENERS

JANET WARRINGTON

FOREWORD

by

Lendon H. Smith, M.D.

 THE CROSSING PRESS / Freedom, California 95019

For my mother—
the first to feed me.
For my father—
who introduced me to fresh spring peas—seven at a time.

Gratitude must be extended to the people who have helped me
with this book: Barbara Wiemer, Terry Herringshaw, Jackie and
Jack Taylor, Linda Ferris Wright, Walt La Tendre and Sally Gundry.
It has taken a lot of energy and unashamedly I have drawn on the
support of these generous people.

Cover illustration and design by Penknife Studios
Illustrations on pages 18, 59, 72, 103, 123 by Penknife Studios.
   all other illustrations by Martha J. Waters
Book design by Martha J. Waters

Printed in the U.S.A.

Library of Congress Cataloging in Publication Data

Warrington, Janet.
   Sweet and natural.

   Includes index.
   1. Desserts. 2. Cookery (Fruit) 3. Sugar-free diet--
Recipes. I. Title.
TX773.W327   641.8'6   82-4962
ISBN 0-89594-073-6   AACR2
ISBN 0-89594-072-8 (pbk.)

Contents

Foreword 7

Introduction 9

Some Nutrition Basics 11

    Carbohydrates 11

    Fats 12

    Protein 13

    Meal Planning 13

    Food Exchanges 14

General Instructions and A Brief Talk about Ingredients 19

Chapter One / Basic Recipes 23

Chapter Two / Yeasted Breads and Teacakes 31

Chapter Three / Quick Breads and Muffins 41

Chapter Four / Cakes 49

Chapter Five / Cookies 63

Chapter Six / Crepes 87

Chapter Seven / Fruits 93

Chapter Eight / Pies 105

Chapter Nine / Puddings 117

Chapter Ten / Beverages 133

Index 138

Foreword

Many cookbooks assume too much. Janet Warrington has found that if she is to change bad eating and cooking habits she must not only motivate the participants to try good foods but also she must make it easy. She spells it out. She tells you exactly what your kitchen needs. She reviews the latest research about sugar, roughage, fats, and protein.

The most difficult part of my job is to get everyone in the family to get off the sugar and white flour which seem to be in every dish served. I try logic ("They use up B vitamins; they wreck the teeth.") and try to scare them ("Your liver will fall out.") or threaten ("I'll double your fees if you get sick.") but nothing works.

Janet has made my job easy. These patients will not have to sacrifice the sweet taste while they give up the sugar bowl. Mother Nature gave us taste buds to detect sweetness and that sensory nerve goes right to the pleasure center of the brain. That drive for sweetness is mainly to get a baby to suck on the breast (milk is sweet) and the older ones to eat fruit when fresh, sweet, and full of vitamin C.

Eating refined sugars is dangerous because they cause the rapid rise and fall of blood sugar and they require another source of B complex vitamins to metabolize them. The intestinal tract will rob the brain and liver of these B's to get the job done; these organs will not function optimally.

The way Janet has arranged for us to get our sweet pleasure satisfied is as close to nature as possible. The sugar is still there but she uses Mother Nature's packaging so it doesn't give the quick rush that the refined products do.

Thank you, Janet. My job is easier now.

—Lendon H. Smith, M.D.

Foreword

Introduction

Making wise choices is what staying healthy and feeling great are all about. General well being depends on selecting fresh fruit, whole grain cookies or slices of whole wheat bread instead of sugary layer cakes. I began making such wise choices when my husband was diagnosed as a diabetic just before our marriage. It was a great shock to me since he was an athlete and was in very good shape. When he was hospitalized, we attended classes together in order to learn as much as we could about his disease and his new diet.

I began reading everything I could lay my hands on, but the more I read, the more confused I became. For instance, we were given a booklet called "Convenience Foods." It listed various foods by brand name along with information as to how they could be worked into a diabetic's diet. It listed an iced chocolate brownie in a portion of 2.2 ounces as equivalent to 2 1/2 Bread Exchanges and 2 Fat Exchanges. This in effect claimed that the brownie was equal in nutrition and in calories to 2 1/2 slices of whole wheat bread and 2 teaspoons of butter. I could never understand how one brownie could have the same vitamins, minerals and fiber as 2 1/2 slices of whole wheat bread spread with 2 teaspoons of butter. I also wondered about the sugar in that brownie, obviously so much more than would be contained in 2 1/2 slices of whole wheat bread. I tried to imagine a person restricted to 6 or 7 Bread Exchanges per day. That brownie would make up 1/3 of the diabetic's total daily allowance. And would the diabetic be able to stop at one brownie? That one brownie would surely act as a bait for the diabetic to overeat, to break the diet.

I came to the realization that refined sugar offers no vitamins, minerals or fiber to diabetics or for that matter to anyone, and I began to search for acceptable alternatives. But every sugar-free cookbook I picked up used either honey or molasses or artificial sweeteners. Honey and molasses act on a diabetic's body the same way sugar does, though they contain trace minerals and vitamins. As for artificial sweeteners, I tried them and found them difficult to bake with and often unpalatable. They are also under question as possible carcinogens.

I had no alternative but to start experimenting in my kitchen to try to produce honey-free, sugar-free, molasses-free, artificial sweeteners-free desserts.

In my searching, I have learned a great deal about nutrition from Dr. Lendon H. Smith, Nikki and David Goldbeck and Joe Gibbons. I also learned a lot from my family.

My grandmothers both loved to cook. I remember waking up on Saturday morning to the smell of something wonderful baking in one grandmother's kitchen. She incorporated cottage cheese, plums, apples, poppy seeds, nuts and golden raisins into many of her breads. My other grandma once sent me home when I was very young with my own small loaf of homemade bread, warm from the oven. Both women taught me about nutritious foods by using a variety of fresh whole ingredients. It was natural to them. I didn't realize the valuable lessons they had given me until later when I was searching for alternatives to baking with sugar.

This book does not advocate serving desserts like pie, cake or cookies every day. Fruits, nuts, cheese and whole grain breads are the best treats for ordinary meals. However, there are times when it's just not a birthday without a cake, when it's just not Christmas without a cookie. These are the times when even the best intentioned cooks have a difficult time finding acceptable alternatives.

These recipes satisfy both our sweet tooth and our sense of celebration—and they are sweet and natural. I hope you enjoy preparing them and eating them.

—Janet Warrington, November 18, 1981

Some Nutrition Basics

CARBOHYDRATES

Carbohydrates are the ideal source of energy; per gram they provide four calories. There are many ways to obtain this energy source, some better than others, because of the nutrients and fiber that come with them. The refined sources of carbohydrates—white flour, sugar, instant rice—have been stripped of their nutrients. They are practically pure starch. The complex carbohydrates, on the other hand, have the advantage of offering certain vitamins, and in whole grains and legumes, amino acids for protein composition. Our bodies require certain vitamins to metabolize carbohydrates for use as fuel. Eating large amounts of refined carbohydrates which supply none of these vitamins would deplete these vitamins from the body. It makes sense to eat those carbohydrates that come in their complex package, complete with vitamins needed for utilization, instead of drawing on the body's vitamin supply to process stripped-down, refined carbohydrates.

The fiber present in whole grains, legumes, fruits and vegetables slow down the digestive process, so that naturally present sugars aren't dumped all at once into the blood stream. This slowed mobility helps avoid those sugar highs and lows experienced by so many. Complex carbohydrates are very satisfying and many people find that they eat less when they switch from refined to complex carbohydrates.

Honey, molasses, raw sugar, brown sugar, fructose, dextrose, maple syrup, invert sugar and corn syrup are all names used for forms of sugar. Honey may be a natural product but it is also very refined. Those bees are efficient little refineries, processing honey. It is almost pure carbohydrate with trace amounts of nutrients that are destroyed by heat. The only advantage of using honey is that it is so very concentrated, so sweet, that less of it can be used.

Many people use honey, molasses, maple syrup, etc. believing that they're getting minerals and/or vitamins. In the case of honey, molasses, brown sugar, and maple syrup, we are at the mercy of the processors. The vitamin and mineral content of these sugars depends on the heat used during production, the method of processing and packaging procedures. Even after very careful handling, the vitamins and minerals are present only in very small amounts.

Lately, a lot of attention has been given to fructose, a form of sugar extracted from fruit. The idea is that fruit is good for you and fructose comes from fruit so . . . But fructose is extracted and purified and, when it gets right down to it, is just another name for sugar. Once a refined sugar enters the blood stream, the body responds by increasing the blood level of insulin. If no fiber, protein or fat is present to slow the breakdown and to level out the blood sugar level, the extra insulin which stimulates the cells to take up the glucose, will produce that low feeling, sometimes reflected by a mood swing, headache or even the shakes. When teaching preschool I witnessed many children experiencing a drop in energy around ten a.m. each morning. My response was a protein snack and a discussion with parents about breakfast cereals.

Sugar has been linked with heart disease, diabetes, dental caries and obesity. Obesity, by the way, is a form of malnutrition, yet in a country where it is widespread, it is generally accepted as mere over-indulgence. The average per person consumption of sugar in the U.S. is about 100 pounds of table sugar and 15 pounds of corn syrup annually. It is laced into almost every convenience food on the market, condiments, luncheon meats, commercial yogurt, peanut butter and canned vegetables, not to mention packaged desserts.

Carbohydrates are not bad; they are essential. We need to make intelligent choices among these foods that provide our source of energy.

FATS

Fats not only make food more palatable—they serve as carriers for vitamins A, D, E and K. They also fill you up. Fat provides energy, with almost two times the amount of calories per gram (9 calories) than carbohydrates or proteins.

Unfortunately, fats are not always visible. High protein foods such as meat, eggs and dairy products are generally high in fat. These are fats that are called saturated, that is they are solid at room temperature. (I always visualize them in my arteries that way too.) Polyunsaturated fats are generally liquid at room temperatures—vegetable oils are polyunsaturated.

Fat consumption has been linked with the great number of overweight people in the United States. Moderate intake is the key to a healthy diet—you should try to keep the percentage of fats in your diet down to 1/3 the total. Nonfat milk can be used in place of whole milk, nonfat yogurt in place of full fat yogurt, yogurt cheese in place of cream cheese.

PROTEIN

Most Americans get more than enough protein. Even vegetarians do not have cause for concern unless they are eating a lot of refined foods.

Each gram of protein consumed provides four calories, about the same as a gram of carbohydrate, less than half of a gram of fat.

What does protein have to do with desserts? Desserts should be included only as a healthful accompaniment to a meal. If the supply of protein in the meal is low, then the dessert should supply the necessary protein. If the supply of protein in the meal is high, the dessert should not include protein. Desserts must be thought through as part of the balanced nutritional package a meal should be.

MEAL PLANNING

Balance is the focus of a healthful diet. A good rule of thumb is to aim for an over-all dietary balance consisting of 30-33 percent calories from fat, 15 percent from protein and 50-55 percent from complex carbohydrates. Dessert should be figured into the balance of the meal.

The calories and exchanges listed with each recipe throughout this book are there to help you in your meal planning. All values are approximate,[1] as all apples, bananas, etc. are not nutritionally identical.

I use *Laurel's Kitchen* and *The Nutrition Almanac* as sources for food value information, and encourage you to secure such a reference and keep it handy in your kitchen or wherever you plan most of your meals. For more specific information on fitting together carbohydrates, proteins and fats, *Feast on a Diabetic Diet*[2] is excellent.

---

[1]Nutrition Composition Tables; Laurel Robertson, Carol Flinders, Bronwen Godfrey, *Laurel's Kitchen,* Nilgiri Press, Berkeley, CA., 1977, p. 458-484; and John D. Kirschmann, director, Nutrition Search Inc., *Nutrition Almanac,* McGraw-Hill Book Co., 1975, p. 185-219, and in a few instances such as with unsweetened coconut and tapioca, nutrition information was acquired directly from food companies.

[2]Joe Gibbons and Euell Gibbons, *Feast on a Diabetic Diet,* Fawcett Publications, Greenwich, Connecticut, 1973.

FOOD EXCHANGES

Food exchanges are simply an expansion of the concept of the Basic Four Food Groups. In the Basic Four, foods are grouped according to the type of nutrients they provide. The Basic Four are: 1) Breads and Cereals, 2) Meats, 3) Dairy Products and 4) Fruits and Vegetables. The Food Exchanges are more specific groupings. They are also categorized by the nutrients that they provide. The categories are: 1) Breads, 2) Fats, 3) Fruits, 4) Meats, 5) Milks and 6) Vegetables. Each food within a group is broken down into a portion that provides a specified amount of protein, carbohydrate and fat (and therefore calories). For example, foods in the Bread Exchange generally provide 2 grams of protein and 15 grams of carbohydrate for a total of about 70 calories. One standard slice of whole wheat bread equals one Bread Exchange, as do 3 cups of popped, no fat added, large-kernel popcorn, 1 small potato, or 1/4 cup wheat germ.

The following is a list of the Food Exchanges.

MAJOR FOOD EXCHANGE LISTS

Bread Exchange
  2 grams protein
  15 grams carbohydrate
  70 calories

Fat Exchange
  5 grams fat
  45 calories

Fruit Exchange
  10 grams carbohydrate
  40 calories

Meat Exchange
Lean:
  7 grams protein
  3 grams fat
  55 calories
Medium:
  7 grams protein
  5 grams fat
  75 calories
High Fat:
  7 grams protein
  8 grams fat
  100 calories

Milk Exchange
Nonfat:
  8 grams protein
  12 grams carbohydrate
  trace fat
  80 calories
Low Fat:
  8 grams protein
  12 grams carbohydrate
  3-5 grams fat
  107-125 calories
Whole Fat:
  8 grams protein
  12 grams carbohydrate
  10 grams fat
  170 calories

Vegetable Exchange
  2 grams protein
  5 grams carbohydrates
  25 calories

The Exchange System has been devised for people on restricted diets by the American Diabetes Association (A.D.A.)[3] and the American Dietetic Association[4] for ease in meal planning. Exchange lists help people on restricted diets plan meals with variety. Each person's daily exchange formula or meal plan is worked out with a trained diet counselor. A person needing 1800 calories per day would have that 1800 calories divided up in a balance of food exchanges. Their daily meal plan would probably look something like this:

7 Bread Exchanges
4 Fruit Exchanges
7 Meat (Medium Fat)* Exchanges
2 1/2 Milk (Low Fat)* Exchanges
2 B-Vegetable Exchanges**
4 Fat Exchanges

Exchanges would be arranged to create breakfast, lunch, dinner and snacks. Individual food habits and daily routine are taken into consideration when the meal planning is done and a balance of proteins, carbohydrates and fats is always the main objective. The meal plan for the above mentioned example might be arranged as follows:

Breakfast: 1 Milk (Low Fat) Exchange
            2 Bread Exchanges
            1 Fat Exchange
            1 Meat (Medium Fat) Exchange
            1 Fruit Exchange

Morning   1 Meat (Medium Fat) Exchange
Snack: 1 Fruit Exchange

Lunch: 2 Bread Exchanges
            2 Meat (Medium Fat) Exchanges
            2 Fat Exchanges
            1 B-Vegetable Exchange

---

[3] American Diabetes Association, Inc. 600 Fifth Ave., New York, N.Y. 10020

[4] The American Dietetic Association, 430 North Michigan Ave., Chicago, Ill. 60611

* The Meat and Milk Exchanges have been further subdivided according to fat content: nonfat, lowfat, medium fat, etc.

** The Vegetable Exchange has been divided into two groups, A and B. A-Vegetables are raw vegetables of negligible caloric value such as parsley, lettuce, endive, watercress, etc. Group B-Vegetables contain more concentrated food value (25 calories per 1/2 cup) such as carrots, broccoli, and tomatoes. The starchy vegetables—corn, peas, limas, potatoes, yams and winter squash—are counted as Bread Exchanges.

| Afternoon | 1 Milk (Low Fat) Exchange |
| Snack: | 1 Fruit Exchange |

Supper:	2 Bread Exchanges
	2 Meat (Medium Fat) Exchange
	1 Fat Exchange
	1 B-Vegetable Exchange
	1 Fruit Exchange

Evening	1 Bread Exchange
Snack:	1 Meat (Medium Fat) Exchange
	1/2 Milk (Low Fat) Exchange

Supplied with this basic format, a person can plan with great variety each days menu. Knowing that the mid-morning snack is 1 Fruit Exchange and 1 Meat (Medium Fat) Exchange, simplifies selection to those items on the Fruit and Meat Exchange Lists. A small apple and an ounce of Farmer Jack Cheese or 1/2 cup of orange juice and a hard boiled egg would constitute interesting snack combinations from the Fruit and Meat Exchange Lists. Knowing from which lists to choose and the number of portions allocated gives a frame of reference for creating each day's meals. For the specific lists of foods within each exchange, write the ADA requesting "Exchange Lists for Meal Planning."

HOW TO FIGURE MY VARIATIONS IN YOUR CHART OF EXCHANGES

Many of my recipes end with suggested variations. Please remember to adjust the nutritional information to fit your variation. For example, if you decide to use sunflower seeds instead of pumpkin seeds, you can use twice as many. All values are approximate.

Nuts and Seeds
1 Fat Exchange (45 calories) =
    almonds—7
    cashews—7
    cashew butter—1/2 tablespoon
    unsweetened coconut, shredded—1 1/2 tablespoons
    peanuts—6
    unsweetened peanut butter—1/2 tablespoon
    pecans—6 halves
    pumpkin seeds—1 tablespoon
    sesame seeds—1 tablespoon
    soy nuts—3 tablespoons
    sunflower seeds—2 1/2 tablespoons

tahini—1 tablespoon
walnuts—6 halves

Cream
1 Fat Exchange (45 calories) =
    cream cheese—1 tablespoon
    sour cream—2 tablespoons
    whipped cream—1 tablespoon

Meals and Flours
1 Bread Exchange (70 calories) =
    bran—1/2 cup
    bran flour—5 tablespoons
    buckwheat flour—3 tablespoons
    dry oatmeal—4 1/2 tablespoons
    carob powder—4 1/2 tablespoons
    rice, cooked—1/2 cup
    soy flour—4 tablespoons
    triticale flour (estimated)—3 tablespoons
    whole wheat flour—3 tablespoons

Milks (Nonfat)
1 Nonfat Milk Exchange (80 calories) =
    milk, skim—1 cup
    milk, dry, nonfat, instant—1/3 cup
    milk, dry, nonfat, non-instant—3 tablespoons
    yogurt, nonfat plain—1 cup

Fruits
1 Fruit Exchange (40 calories) =
    apple—1 small (2 1/2-inches diameter)
    apple juice, unsweetened—1/3 cup
    applesauce, unsweetened—1/2 cup
    applebutter, unsweetened—2 tablespoons
    apricots, dried—3 halves
    banana—1/2 small (7 3/4-inch)
    blackberries—1/2 cup
    blueberries—1/2 cup
    cantaloupe—1/4 of 6-inch diameter melon
    cherries, sweet—10 large
    cherries, sour—1/2 cup
    dates—2 medium, pitted
    figs, dried—1 large
    grapefruit, unsweetened—1/2 medium
    grapefruit juice—1/2 cup
    grapes, Thompson seedless—12
    grape juice, unsweetened—1/4 cup
    honeydew melon—1/4 of small

nectarine—1 medium
orange—1 small
orange juice, unsweetened—1/2 cup
peach—1 medium
peach, dried—1 large half
pear—1 small
pear, dried—1 medium half
pineapple, fresh—1/2 cup
pineapple, canned, unsweetened—1/2 cup
pineapple juice, unsweetened—1/3 cup
plums—2 medium, 3 small
prunes—2 large
prune juice, unsweetened—1/4 cup
raisins—2 tablespoons
raspberries—1/2 cup
strawberries—3/4 cup
watermelon—3/4 cup

General Instructions
and
A Brief Talk about Ingredients

GENERAL TIPS

FRAME OF MIND
   If you habitually sweeten your food with sugar, honey or chemicals, give your tongue and taste buds a while to go through withdrawal. It's amazing how they come around and wake up to naturally sweet flavors.

SELECTING INGREDIENTS
   Fresh is best—always. Don't start with bad fruit or poor ingredients. If you must use canned fruits, use those packed in water or in their own juice.

PROCEDURE
   Read through a recipe to see what needs chopping, slicing, etc. I prefer to do all of my chopping first and then assemble all the ingredients. It's a systematic approach that works well for me.

STORAGE
   Don't store baked goods in aluminum pans in your refrigerator. They taste like metal and seem to spoil quickly. Wrap things in plastic wrap or airtight containers. Most of these recipes freeze well, especially the breads and cookies. Some of the cookies can even be frozen before baking (i.e. Kiflis, page 64).

INGREDIENTS

BANANAS
   To ripen bananas, place them in a brown bag, and keep them at room temperature in a dark place, such as a cupboard for several days.
   In my recipes *ripe* means a banana that is mostly yellow with several brown speckled areas; whereas, *very ripe* indicates a banana that is more brown than yellow.

BANANA EQUIVALENTS

A.   A small banana=about 7 3/4-inches in length
2 1/4 small bananas = 1 cup mashed banana
2 small bananas = 1 cup sliced bananas

B.   A medium banana = about 8 3/4-inches in length
2 medium bananas = 1 cup mashed banana
1 4/5 medium bananas = 1 cup sliced banana

C.   A large banana = about 9 3/4-inches in length
1 4/5 large bananas = 1 cup mashed banana
1 1/2 large bananas = 1 cup sliced banana

CAROB

Carob has a delightfully gentle flavor. It's naturally sweeter than cocoa, lower in fat and contains no caffeine. It grows in long brown pods on evergreen trees in the Mediterranean. The carob pods are also referred to as St. John's bread, named after John the Baptist. Legend has it that he lived on honey and locust beans while travelling and preaching. The carob pods, confused with locust pods, were dubbed St. John's Bread.

For chocolate connoisseurs, carob is unsatisfactory as a substitute. Avoid introducing carob as "just like chocolate." In fact, to avoid disappointment, when I name my carob desserts, I steer clear of any indication of chocolate. For instance, carob bars are never referred to as brownies and carob chiffon pie is never "chocolate cream pie." Carob has a distinctive flavor that should be appreciated on its own merit. It is sold as carob powder or carob flour in most health food stores.

CHEESE

Cheese: Real cheese is white or ivory in color. It is called cheese, not cheese food or cheese product. It has no sugar added and is superb in tea cakes and with apple or cherry dishes.

Cheese and fruit make a gourmet dessert, simple and delicious. The following cheeses make excellent dessert cheeses:

Brie	Pallatelle
Camembert	Petit Swisse
Cheddar	Port Salute
Edam	Swiss
Gouda	Yogurt Cheese
Gruyere	

Cheese is most flavorful at room temperature, so set it out for at least 30 minutes before serving time.

FLOURS

Steer clear of refined white flour. It doesn't have much personality and has been stripped of many of its valuable nutrients and fiber. When white flour is called for, use unbleached; it has been exposed to a little less processing than bleached white flour. Most of my recipes use all whole wheat or whole wheat and soy flour combinations. Wheat flour contains more of the whole wheat berry than white flour does. The bran and wheat germ are the brown parts of this flour. It gives a rich nutty flavor and full chewy texture to your baked goods. When unbleached flour is called for, it is used in combination with whole wheat and serves a specific purpose, such as ease in handling.

Soy flour is made from cooked and dried soybeans that have been finely ground. Use soy flour only in baked or heated products; eating raw soy flour will inhibit digestion of protein (it contains an enzyme that will do this). Compared to wheat flours, soy flour is low in carbohydrates and high in protein, making it a convenient way to improve the protein content of baked goods. However, because soy flour lacks gluten, if used overenthusiastically, it will produce very heavy cakes and breads.

Most of my recipes use 2-4 tablespoons soy flour to one cup of wheat flour.

GELATIN

Gelatin: Unflavored gelatin is an animal product that is useful in preparing pies and puddings. It contains some protein but it is not digestible protein, or a complete protein. Therefore, it is not an adequate protein source. For those persons preferring not to use animal products, there is another gelling substance that comes from the sea, called agar. Agar is available in flakes or sticks and is quite simple to use. For example, fruit gelatins can be made by providing 2 tablespoons of agar flakes for every cup of fruit juice. Boil the juice and agar together, then simmer for two or three minutes, stirring occasionally. Add nuts, sliced or chopped fruit and refrigerate until set.

GRAINS

Rice, Oats: Use whole raw brown rice and old fashioned rolled oats. The instant varieties have the same problem as refined white flour. They are processed foods.

Triticale: Triticale flakes are made from a cereal grain called triticale. It is cross bred rye and wheat. The protein value of triticale is 16 percent higher than most other cereal grains. Triticale flakes are mentioned only in my Granola recipe (page 70). However, I like to keep a mixture of oats, triticale and wheat flakes on hand as a desirable substitute in any recipe calling for rolled oats such as Raisin Drops (page 83).

MILK

Dry Milk: I prefer non-instant, nonfat milk simply because it has been processed less than instant, and seems to taste a little sweeter.

I supplement many of my recipes with dry milk for the same reasons that I use soy flour—to give foods a nutritive boost. It also gives a nice soft texture to homebaked breads.

To reconstitute 1 quart of non-instant nonfat milk, use your blender, combining 2/3 cup milk with 4 cups water.

SWEET SPICES

The sweet spices (nutmeg, ginger, cinnamon, cloves and allspice) have a special shelf in my kitchen. These spices and the vanilla and almond extracts can greatly enhance the sweetness of the desserts you prepare. They should never overwhelm a dish unless they are the featured flavor (i.e. Gingerbread Cookies, page 80). Following is a list of combinations that I find personally pleasing. You may wish to experiment; use your nose and your imagination.

Spice/Fruit Combinations

Almond extract: bananas, berries, cherries
Allspice: bananas, blueberries, peaches
Cinnamon: apples, berries, peaches, pears, plums
Cloves: apples, blueberries, oranges
Ginger: bananas, pineapple
Nutmeg: apples, bananas, blueberries, oranges, peaches, pears
Vanilla extract: apples, bananas, peaches, pears

CHAPTER ONE
Basic Recipes

Basic Recipes are homemade foods that are used in the preparation of some desserts. Many of these foods such as Unsweetened Applesauce or Nonfat Yogurt can be found ready-made at the store. In my opinion, they taste better when they are homemade. Other recipes such as Sweet Milk, Raisin Maple Syrup and Yogurt Cheese are items that have been developed as thoughtful alternatives to sweetened condensed milk, pancake syrup and cream cheese.

Lecithin/Oil and Blended Butter are handy to prepare in quantity ahead of time so that they're ready for immediate use.

Apple Butter

Preparation time	about 4 hours
Yield	1 1/2 cups

Ingredients

6 very ripe, medium apples (2 1/2-inch diameter)
Use Grimes Golden, Winesap, Jonathons, Cortlands or
other baking apples.
1/2 cup water
1 tsp. cider vinegar
1/2 tsp. cinnamon

1. Thoroughly wash apples, especially near core and blossom end.
2. Core apples and if they've been waxed, peel them.
3. Cut apples into 1-inch chunks.
4. Combine apples and water in heavy bottomed saucepan and heat to boiling.
5. Stir, lower heat and cover.
6. Simmer over low heat, stirring occasionally.
7. When apples are soft, mash them.
8. Stir in vinegar and cinnamon.
9. Continue simmering, over low heat, uncovered, for three or four hours, stirring every half hour or so to prevent sticking.
10. When very thick, remove from heat, cool to room temperature. Refrigerate or freeze for long term storage.

Nutritional information 1 T. = 16 calories or 1/2 fruit exchange

Applesauce

Preparation time 45 minutes
Yield 2 1/2 cups

Ingredients about 5-6 medium (2 1/2-inch diameter), very ripe apples
(Use Grimes Golden, McIntosh, Cortland, Spartan or other
sweet baking apples.)
1/2 cup water

1. Thoroughly wash apples, especially near core and blossom end.
2. Core apples and if they've been waxed, peel them.
3. Chop apples into one inch pieces and pack into measuring cup.
   You should have 4 cups (1 quart) packed, chopped apples.
4. In heavy bottomed saucepan (not aluminum) heat water and
   chopped apples to boiling, stirring occasionally.
5. Lower heat, stir, cover and simmer over low until soft.
6. For chunky applesauce, mash soft apples to desired consistency.
7. For smooth applesauce press soft apples through a foodmill or
   puree in blender.
8. Cool and refrigerate or freeze for long term storage.

Nutritional information per 1/2 cup, 45 calories or 1 fruit exchange

Quick Apricot Butter

Preparation time 20 minutes
Yield 7/8 cup

Ingredients 1/2 cup packed dried, pitted apricot halves
boiling water

1. Measure 1/2 cup apricot halves and place them in a 1 cup
   measuring cup.
2. Fill measuring cup to the 1 cup mark with boiling water.
   Cover with a plate.
3. Steep to soften 10 minutes or longer.
4. Pour water and apricots into the blender and puree until
   smooth.
5. Refrigerate in covered container.

Nutritional information per T.: 12 calories or 1/3 fruit exchange

Blended Butter

I do not use one hundred percent butter in my cooking, which is saturated fat, or margarine which is polyunsaturated but generally contains food color and/or preservatives and is usually highly processed (i.e. hydrogenated). I use blended butter which is simple to make and is spreadable from the refrigerator. If you miss the serving tubs from store-bought margarine, try using your sugar bowl. It's a good size and even has a lid. Use blended butter as you would margarine or butter, keeping in mind that it's as caloric as either and should be used sparingly.

Preparation time 10 minutes
Yield 2 cups

Ingredients **1 cup light oil (safflower or sunflower)**
1 cup good quality sweet butter, room temperature

1. Measure and pour oil into blender.
2. Add butter and blend on high speed until smooth and creamy.
3. Pour into serving dish (sugar bowls, cheese pots, custard cups, mugs).
4. Cover and refrigerate until ready to use. It will solidify but be spreadable from the refrigerator.
5. Many of my recipes call for oil and butter. If you have Blended Butter on hand, you may wish to use it instead. For example, if a recipe uses 1/4 cup oil, and 1/4 cup butter, then use 1/2 cup Blended Butter.

Nutritional information per tsp., 45 calories or 1 fat exchange

Lecithin/Oil

Are you familiar with liquid lecithin? It's a soybean derivative that acts as an emulsifier, breaking down fat. This dark, viscous liquid is terrific when combined with oil for preparing loaf and cake pans, muffin cups and baking sheets. It takes very little lecithin/oil to do the job that would usually require 1 tablespoon of grease or oil. I even rub a little of it on my hands and bread board before kneading whole wheat bread, and have coated my dough hook with it for easy dough removal. After being baked in a lecithin/oil prepared pan, cakes and breads literally leave the pan without losing a crumb. It also darkens metal pans and baking sheets for even browning of breads and cookies.

For persons who must count fats used in food preparation, this offers an alternative that eliminates more than 2/3's of the fat used in oiling or greasing pans, and no flouring is necessary.

Lecithin can also be used as an egg substitute in breads. One tablespoon of lecithin in place of one egg per loaf gives a nice smooth texture; however, no more than one tablespoon per loaf should be used as it will then affect flavor. Liquid lecithin is available in most natural food stores and a little goes a long way.

Ingredients
2 parts pure liquid lecithin
1 part light oil (sunflower, safflower)

1. Using a funnel, or a very steady hand, pour 2 parts lecithin to 1 part oil into a small plastic squeeze bottle.
2. Cap and refrigerate.
3. Use lecithin/oil at room temperature as it becomes very thick when refrigerated.
4. Shake or roll the bottle before using it to combine the oil and lecithin.
5. Use lecithin/oil sparingly. I find it takes less than 1 teaspoon per loaf pan or cookie sheet.

Sweet Milk

Sweet Milk: Naturally sweet, this milk is delicious on cold or hot cereals and grains. It is also a common ingredient in many of my desserts. I like to keep a jar of it hanging around in my refrigerator for spur of the moment baking. It should be made at least one day in advance of use, but reaches peak sweetness after two or three days.

Ingredients

2 cups reconstituted nonfat milk
2/3 cup raisins

1. Combine milk and raisins in a jar, cover and refrigerate at least overnight.
2. Before using, shake the jar vigorously. Milk should be an ivory color.
3. Strain the milk to remove the raisins which will be mushy and a little flat tasting.
4. Use milk as directed.

Raisin Maple Syrup

Delicious brushed over baked apples or apple dumplings. It's very sweet so use parsimoniously!

Preparation time   20 minutes
Yield   about 1 cup

Ingredients

1 cup raisins
1/4 cup water
1 T. Blended Butter (see page 26) or
    1/2 T. butter and 1/2 T. oil
1-2 teaspoons maple extract, as desired

1. In a saucepan, heat raisins, water and butter until butter melts and raisins plump.
2. Processing 1/3 cup at a time, blend the hot raisin mixture on high speed.
3. Return pureed raisins to the saucepan and simmer until it reaches desired consistency.
4. Remove from heat and stir in maple extract flavoring, as desired.

Nonfat Yogurt

Preparation time 30 minutes to prepare, 4-8 hours to incubate
Yield 2 quarts

When people ask me if I have a yogurt maker, I smile and say "yes . . . me!" This lowfat yogurt is simple to make and requires very little preparation time. The yogurt culture does most of the work. The success of your yogurt depends upon your attending to milk and water temperatures. Your job is to provide a comfortable growing environment for the culture. If milk or water is too hot, the culture will be killed. If these liquids are too cool, the lactobacilli will get lazy and grow slowly or not at all.

Supplies
1 deep kettle
1 2-quart kettle
2 1-quart jars with lids
thermometer (deep fry) that registers 110-120 degrees
2 2/3 cups nonfat dry milk
7 1/2 cups warm water
4 tablespoons yogurt from last batch or commercial lowfat
  plain yogurt

1. In a 2-quart kettle whip together dry milk and water.
2. Heat the milk to 115 degrees F.
3. Pour milk into quart jars and stir 2 tablespoons yogurt into each. Cover each jar securely with lids.
4. Fill a large kettle with hot (117 degrees F.) water. If your tap water isn't this hot, heat it until it registers 117 degrees on your thermometer.
5. Set jars in the kettle of hot water. Water should cover the jars.
6. Cover the kettle and set it in the oven. If you have a gas oven the pilot will provide enough incubation heat (80 degrees). If you have an electric oven, turn on the oven light to provide incubation heat. Or, if you prefer, set the covered kettle on a double thickness of towels and wrap the whole thing with one large thick towel.
7. Let yogurt culture do its work for at least 4 hours. Those little bacteria may take longer if the environment is colder than 80 degrees. Generally, I let mine work overnight.
8. Yogurt should appear smooth and pull away from jar side completely when tipped. It will have a little whey on top.
9. Refrigerate yogurt until ready to use.

Nutritional information per cup, 80 calories or 1 milk exchange (nonfat)

Yogurt Cheese

This creamy spread is a fine lowfat alternative to cream cheese. Just try it on banana bread, or serve a small amount on a plate with sliced fruit.

Preparation time   5 minutes to prepare, 12-16 hours to drain
Yield   about 1/2 cup or 24 teaspoons

Ingredients
1 cup nonfat plain yogurt
cheesecloth
string

1. Fold cheesecloth into a 10-inch square, 4 layers thick.
2. Spoon lowfat plain yogurt onto the center of the square of cheesecloth.
3. Draw up the sides and corners to make a bag. Tie the string around the bag ends securely.
4. Hang this cheese bag over the sink or a bowl to drain. You may want to secure it to the faucet. It is important that the yogurt has drip space, don't set it in or on anything.
5. Allow yogurt to drip/drain for 12-16 hours.
6. Carefully open cheese bag and with a spoon scrape up the yogurt cheese and transfer it to a small bowl.
7. Whip the yogurt cheese for a minute, then transfer it to a serving dish or cup. Refrigerate covered.

Nutritional information   per teaspoon, 3 calories

Yogurt Cheese Icing

For youngsters who turn down cake that isn't iced, try combining Yogurt Cheese with pureed fruit to make a lowfat frosting. Add enough fruit to make it spreadable. Then thinly spread over cake before serving.

CHAPTER TWO
Yeasted Breads and Tea Cakes

Whole Wheat Bread

This light and chewy bread is a treat by itself, sliced and spread with butter. It can also be shaped into tea cakes. The recipes follow.

If you have a mixer or processor with dough hooks this bread will take about 90 minutes from start to finish. If you are kneading by hand it will take about two hours longer for the extra rising time.

Bread baking should be done when you have the time and are in a creative spirit. It warms a kitchen like no other activity.

Yield 2 large or 3 small loaves

Ingredients
1/3 cup packed, pitted dates
2 1/2 cups warm water
1/4 cup nonfat dry milk
2 T. yeast
1/4 tsp. vitamin C (ascorbic acid—grind a vitamin C tablet)
1 T. salt
3/8 cup sunflower or safflower oil
2 large eggs, lightly beaten
1/3 cup lowfat soy flour
6 1/2 cups finely ground whole wheat flour

1. All ingredients should be at room temperature when you begin. In a blender, puree on high speed, dates, water and dry milk.
2. Proceed using Dough Hook Method or Hand Kneaded Method.

Dough Hook Method
3. Pour milk-date mixture into bowl of the mixer/processor. Add yeast and let it sit for five minutes. This gives the yeast time to bud. Hope for energetic yeast!
4. Meanwhile oil two 9 x 5 x 3 inch loaf pans or three 8½ x 4½ x 2½ inch loaf pans.

5. With mortar and pestle, or the back of a spoon, grind up a vitamin C tablet to equal 1/4 tsp. (Or you can purchase the powdered form of vitamin C to eliminate grinding your own.) The vitamin C facilitates the yeast.

6. Add vitamin C, salt, oil and soy flour to budding yeast, stir briefly.

7. Turn mixer on high and add 4 cups of the finely ground whole wheat flour. Beat for 2 minutes.

8. Add 2-2 1/2 cups additional whole wheat flour as mixer is running on high. When dough begins pulling from sides, turn mixer down to low. Knead with the mixer on low for ten minutes.

9. Preheat oven to 175 degrees (warm).

10. Prepare bread board and hands with oil or lecithin.

11. Turn out dough and divide into two pieces. Set one piece aside.

12. Shape dough into a ball, flatten to a large rectangle, fold into thirds,

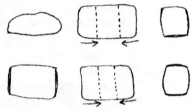

turn, flatten, fold into thirds again, pinch seam side and place seam side down in prepared pan.

13. Repeat step 12 with the other half of the dough.

14. Place bread in 175 degree (warm) oven for 30 minutes, turn oven up to 300 degrees for 20 minutes, then finish baking at 350 degrees for 15-20 minutes or until bread sounds hollow when tapped.

15. Remove bread from pan and rest it on its side to cool. Let it cool one hour before slicing or wrapping as it continues to bake on the inside until cool. Resting it on its side results in a lighter loaf than sitting it on its top or bottom because of the combination of the internal baking that continues until it's cool and the natural force of gravity.

16. When bread has cooled completely, wrap and store in an air-tight container. This bread makes delicious toast. This bread freezes well.

17. To heat frozen bread, plan ahead and wrap bread in foil before freezing. Then 20-30 minutes before serving it, heat foil-wrapped bread at 350 degrees.

Hand Kneaded Method

3. Pour milk-date mixture into a large bowl. Add yeast and let it set for five minutes, giving the yeast time to bud. Hope for energetic yeast!

4. Meanwhile, oil two 8½ x 4½ x 2½ inch loaf pans.

5. With mortar and pestle or the back of a spoon, grind up a vitamin C tablet to equal 1/4 tsp. ascorbic acid. Or you can purchase the powdered form to eliminate grinding your own. The vitamin C facilitates the yeast.
6. Add vitamin C, salt, oil and soy flour to budding yeast, stir briefly.
7. Stir in 4 cups of finely ground whole wheat flour and beat vigorously with a wooden spoon, about 200 strokes.
8. Beat in an additional 2 cups whole wheat flour. When it gets too stiff to beat, mix with your hands, working the flour in to make a soft, elastic dough.
9. Turn dough out onto a floured board and knead in up to 1/2 cup more flour. Turn and fold dough, flatten to a rectangle, pull ends together, form a baby's bottom, push down with knuckles, take out your frustrations, push in your good feelings and think about how tremendous this bread will smell baking. Knead for a good ten minutes; bread should be responsive to your touch—the yeast cells are cooperating! Pull ends together and form a large ball. Set aside.
10. To provide a warm rising environment, turn on the oven light, unless your oven is gas, then the pilot will provide enough heat.
11. Prepare a large bowl with oil or lecithin.
12. Place dough into prepared bowl, turning once to lightly coat top with lecithin/oil. Cover dough with a dampened clean towel and place bowl in closed oven (light on).
13. Let dough rise for 1 1/2 -2 hours or until doubled in bulk.
14. Prepare board and hands with lecithin/oil or oil. Turn out dough and divide into 2 pieces. Set one piece aside.
15. Preheat oven to 175 degrees (warm).
16. Proceed using steps 12-17, Dough Hook Method.

Variation   Raisin Bread: Knead in 1/2 cup raisins per loaf. Roll dough out into a large rectangle, sprinkle with cinnamon and roll up. Place in loaf pan seam side down and bake as directed.

Nutritional information   per slice, 70 calories or 1 bread exchange

Tea Cakes

Preparation time 15 minutes to shape, 40-45 minutes to bake

Use the preceeding recipe or any bread dough which you like.
The recipes for fillings follow the instructions for assembling the
tea cakes.

Assembling Tea Cake # 1
Yield One 9-inch round coffee cake

Let bread rise once, in oiled bowl for 1 hour or until doubled in
bulk. Punch down and pinch off about 6-8 ounces. Roll it into
a circle and flatten it into an oiled 9-inch round cake pan. Brush
with melted butter. Bring dough up sides of pan an inch or so.
Fill.
    Pinch off another 6-8 ounces of dough. Divide this into 4
pieces. Roll each piece out, like a snake, and (a) cross them in
the pan over filling. Pinch dough "snakes" together at the center
and at the sides of the pan. Or you can (b) weave dough snakes.
Or (c) twist them into any shape that pleases you—arranging
them around the edge or over the filling. You may want to just
(d) flatten the top—just like the bottom—and cut slits in it.

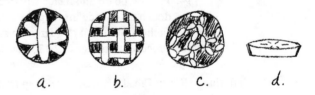

a.   b.   c.   d.

Tea Cake # 2 Take 14-16 ounces of dough that has risen once. Roll it out into
a rectangle and spread filling over it. Roll it up and slice it into
8 or so pieces. Arrange these on an oiled pan—the size depends
on how much dough and filling you use. Let rise 30-40 minutes.
Bake at 350 degrees for 45 minutes or so.

Tea Cake # 3   Take 16-20 ounces of dough that has risen once. Roll it into a rectangle and spread filling over it. Roll it up carefully and gently place it into an oiled tube pan—seam side down. Pinch ends gently to seal. Bake at 350 degrees for 1 hour or so.

bird's eye view

Sweet Rolls   Do what you did for Tea Cake # 2 only separate pieces on a lecithin/oil prepared cookie sheet. Use about 1 ounce of dough per roll.

    OR: Flatten 1 ounce of dough into a circle, put a spoonful of filling in center and bring sides up, pinching together. Turn your creation over and place it on a prepared sheet or in a prepared baking dish, i.e. Filled Rolls (p. 38). If you like them soft, put them close together so that when they raise, they'll touch and bake together. If you like them chewy, put them further apart—so the heat will circulate and crispen the outside of each. Bake at 350 degrees for 25 minutes or so.

Tea Cake Fillings

Apple/Pear   1. Combine 2 cups sliced apples (thinly sliced) with currants or raisins, cinnamon, nutmeg and walnuts.

Berry   2. Two cups fresh berries—gently mashed with spices of your choice. Cook over high heat, stirring constantly until thickened. (See Sweet Spices.)

Peach   3. Peach Filling—chop 2 cups peaches, place over high heat. Cook, stirring, until thickened. Add cinnamon and some chopped nuts.

Pineapple   4. Use crushed or chunk pineapple—cook down as for Peach Filling—add coconut or chopped pecans, omit cinnamon—use a pinch of ginger if you like.

Dried Fruits   5. Chop up dates, apples, raisins, prunes, or apricots—or any combination. For 8 ounces dried fruit, add 4 ounces water. Cook on high, stirring and mashing gently until you like the consistency. Cool it. Add vanilla (or almond) extract and chopped nuts (or coconut).

Nut   6. Grind 2 cups of nuts—a combination or just one type—use unsalted ones. You may want to add some sunflower seeds too. Stir in cinnamon and nutmeg. Add 1/2 tsp. of almond or vanilla extract. To aid the consistency you may want to add an egg white.

Poppy Seed   7. Grind 1/2 cup poppy seed with mortar and pestle or spice grinder. Add a dash of cinnamon and enough pureed fruit (berry, cherry or grape seems best) to bind it to a spreading consistency (about 1/2 cup). This is delicious—but make sure you brush your teeth if you're going to meet the Queen.

Cheese-Fruit   8. Grate or shred 2 ounces of cheddar, swiss or your favorite natural cheese (real, unprocessed, uncolored). Combine it with 1/2 cup of chopped fresh or dried fruit. This one is not easy to work with. It is not recommended for any rolls that have to be handled a lot.

     The cheese will melt around the fruit and help keep your bread moist. Make sure you refrigerate these.

Cottage Cheese   9. Combine 1 cup cottage cheese or ricotta with cinnamon and golden raisins or other chopped dry fruit. (My grandmother used dried cottage cheese—you can substitute drained cottage cheese—mixed with golden raisins.)

Apricot Bread/Rolls

Delicious toasted or warm from the oven.

Preparation time 1 1/2 hours
Yield 1 large loaf or 28 rolls

Ingredients **1/2 recipe Whole Wheat Bread**
1 cup chopped dried apricots
1/2 cup chopped pecans, almonds or walnuts

1. Prepare Whole Wheat Bread as recipe on page 31 directs. Before shaping into a loaf, however, knead in the chopped apricots and nuts.
2. Shape into a loaf or rolls (#3 above). Place loaf into an oiled loaf pan and bake as Whole Wheat Bread recipe directs.
3. To make rolls: pinch off 1 ounce of dough and roll it into a round, smooth ball. Repeat this with all of the dough and place the rolls, sides touching, into a lecithin/oil prepared 9 x 13 inch baking dish. Bake at 175 degrees for 15 minutes, 300 degrees for 15 minutes and 350 degrees for 20-25 minutes or until browned and test done.
4. Cool bread to room temperature before wrapping.
5. These freeze well.

Nutritional information per slice/roll, 90 calories, 1 bread, 1/4 fruit and 1/4 fat exchange

Filled Rolls

Preparation time	3 hours
Yield	24 rolls

Ingredients

3 1/4 cups whole wheat flour
1/4 cup lowfat soy flour
2 T. dry milk
2 T. dry yeast
1/2 tsp. salt
1/4 cup packed pitted dates
3/4 cup water
1/3 cup light oil, sunflower or safflower
2 large eggs

Filling

1/2 cup plus 2 T. packed, chopped, pitted* prunes
1/2 cup plus 2 T. chopped almonds
pinch cloves

1. All ingredients should be at room temperature when you begin for optimal yeast budding.
2. In a large bowl combine 1 cup of the whole wheat flour with soy flour, dry milk, yeast and salt. Set aside.
3. Pour 3/4 cup water into the blender, add dates, oil and eggs, processing until dates are finely chopped.
4. Add blender mixture to dry ingredients. Beat well.
5. Beat in 1 1/4 cups whole wheat flour. Beat for 2 minutes on high speed, scraping bowl.
6. Stir in enough additional whole wheat flour (1 cup) to make a soft dough.
7. Knead until smooth and elastic, about 10 minutes.
8. Place dough in an oiled bowl, turning once to coat the top.
9. Cover with a clean damp cloth and let rise in a warm place, free from draft. The inside of a gas oven or electric oven with the oven light on, to provide a little heat, works well for bread rising. Dough should almost double in bulk after 1 hour. Meanwhile make filling.
   To make filling: finely chop pitted prunes and almonds. If desired, add a pinch of cloves. Toss together with a fork. Set aside until dough is ready to shape.
10. Punch down dough and divide it into 24 equal pieces.
11. Roll each piece into a ball, then with the heel of your hand flatten the dough into about a 4 inch circle.
12. Place 1/2 T. filling in the center of each circle.
13. Pull edges of dough up around filling, pinching together to seal.
14. Place rolls, pinched side down, in lecithin/oil prepared muffin cups.

15. Let rise in oven, warmed by pilot or oven light, for 50 minutes or until doubled in bulk.
16. Turn oven on to 350 degrees and bake rolls for 15-20 minutes or until golden (and the kitchen smells terrific).
17. Remove from muffin cups to cool.
18. These freeze well.

*For Easy Prune Pitting Gently steam prunes over boiling water. If you have no steamer, a strainer can be placed over a pan of boiling water. Put the prunes in the strainer or steamer and cover. Steam for about 5-10 minutes. Allow prunes to cool before handling.

Feel each prune for the pit, and with a paring knife, slice into the prune on the pit's edge, peeling the fruit away from the pit.

Variations
Other Ideas for Fillings
1. Combine 1/2 cup plus 2 T. Quick Apricot Butter (see page 25) with 1/2 cup plus 2 T. chopped nuts.
2. Combine 1/2 cup plus 2 T. Apple Butter (see page 24) with 1/2 cup plus 2 T. grated cheddar cheese.

Nutritional information per roll, 132 calories, 1 bread, 1 fat and 1/4 meat (high fat) exchanges

Prune and Cheese Bread

Preparation time   2 hours to prepare and bake
Yield   2 large or 3 small loaves (about 50 slices)

Ingredients
2 T. dry yeast
2 1/2 cups warm water
1 cup pitted prunes (about 20 large)
1 large egg
1/4 tsp. ascorbic acid (1 vitamin C tablet)
1 T. salt
1 cup (4 ounces) coarsely grated aged white Cheddar
1 cup chopped walnuts
1/3 cup lowfat soy flour
5 1/2 cups whole wheat flour

1. In a large mixing bowl dissolve yeast in 1 cup warm water. Set aside.
2. Meanwhile, in blender, puree prunes with 1 egg and 1 1/2 cups water.
3. Add prune mixture to dissolved yeast.
4. Stir in 1 ground vitamin C tablet (1/4 tsp. ascorbic acid); this aids rising.
5. Stir in salt, cheese and chopped walnuts.
6. On high speed of mixer beat in 1/3 cup soy flour and 3 1/2 cups whole wheat flour. Beat for 2 minutes.
7. On low speed beat in 2 cups additional whole wheat flour. If dough becomes too stiff to beat, knead in additional flour by hand.
8. Knead bread for 10 minutes. If bread is too sticky to handle, oil your hands and kneading surface.
9. Prepare two large or three small loaf pans with oil.
10. Preheat oven to 175 degrees (F), warm.
11. Divide dough into two or three equal pieces and shape into loaves.
12. To shape into loaf: flatten dough and shape into a large rectangle, bring both ends in, slap layered dough against bread board, flatten again, bringing opposite sides in this time, folding one over the other. Tuck ends and place loaf, seam side down, in loaf pan. Repeat with the other loaf(s).
13. Bake at 175 degrees for 30 minutes, then raise heat to 300 degrees, baking for 25 minutes. Loaf should do most of rising during this stage of the baking. Finish baking at 350 degrees for 20 minutes or until bread is brown and sounds hollow when tapped on the bottom.
14. Tip loaves out of baking pans and cool them on their sides for no less than 1 hour.
15. Refrigerate, tightly wrapped. Freeze extras.

Nutritional information   per slice, 79 calories or 1 bread exchange

CHAPTER THREE

Quick Breads and Muffins

Banana Bread

Preparation time	2 hours to prepare and bake (prepare Sweet Milk at least 1 day ahead)
Yield	1 loaf or 24 slices

Ingredients

1/4 cup light oil
1/4 cup butter
1/4 cup Sweet Milk (see page 28)
1/4 cup packed pitted dates (about 10)
3 small (7 3/4 inches) or 2 large (9 3/4 inches) very ripe
    bananas
1 large egg
1 1/4 cup whole wheat flour
1/4 cup lowfat soy flour
1/4 cup nonfat dry milk
1 tsp. baking soda
1/2 tsp. salt
1/2 cup raisins
1/2 cup chopped walnuts

1. Combine in blender: oil, butter, sweet milk, dates, bananas and egg. Blend until smooth and dates are chopped fine. Set aside.
2. Preheat oven to 350 degrees (F).
3. Oil a loaf pan and set aside.
4. In a large mixing bowl combine flours, dry milk, baking soda and salt.
5. Beat in blended banana mixture.
6. Stir in raisins and nuts.
7. Pour into loaf pan.
8. Bake at 350 degrees for 60 minutes or until richly browned, kitchen smells great and inserted cake tester comes out clean.
9. Allow bread to cool 10 minutes in the pan before removing.
10. Remove from pan and tip loaf on side. Let cool to room temperature before slicing.
11. Store in an airtight container or wrap in foil and freeze.

Nutritional information   per slice (1/24 of recipe), 107 calories or 1 bread and 1 fat exchange

Brown Bread

Preparation time	2 hours to prepare and bake
Yield	1 round loaf or 28 slices

Ingredients

2 T. dry yeast
1/2 cup warm water
1 large egg
1 cup packed pitted dates (about 40)
1 1/2 cups strong decaffinated coffee, cooled
1 T. grated orange rind
1 T. salt
2 cups rye flour
4 cups whole wheat flour

1. Preheat oven to 175 degrees (F).
2. In a large mixing bowl dissolve yeast in warm water. Set aside.
3. Meanwhile, combine in blender: egg, dates and coffee. Puree until mixture appears uniform.
4. Add blender mixture to dissolved yeast.
5. Stir in orange rind and salt.
6. On high speed beat in 2 cups rye flour and 2 cups whole wheat flour. Beat for 2 minutes.
7. On low speed beat in an additional 2 cups whole wheat flour. If necessary, stop mixer and work in the additional flour by hand.
8. Knead dough for 10 minutes. If it's too sticky to handle, oil your hands and the kneading surface.
9. Prepare a large baking sheet with lecithin/oil or oil.
10. Shape dough into a round, slightly flattened ball and center it on the prepared baking sheet. With a very sharp knife slash a deep X in the top. (Or use this dough in preparation of tea cakes or other filled breads).
11. Bake at 175 degrees for 35 minutes, then at 300 degrees for 25 minutes. Bake at 350 degrees for 25 minutes more or until bread sounds hollow when underside is tapped.
12. Cool to room temperature for at least one hour.
13. Store bread in an airtight container.
14. This bread freezes well.

Nutritional information   per 1 slice (1/28 of recipe), 106 calories or 1 1/2 bread exchange

Zucchini Bread

Delicately flavored, delightful with a cup of tea.

Preparation time 30 minutes, 70 minutes to bake
Yield 1 loaf or 24 servings

Ingredients
1 5-inch zucchini squash
1 1/2 cups whole wheat flour
2 T. lowfat soy flour
2 T. nonfat dry milk powder
   or 2 T. soy flour (for milk free diets)
1 tsp. baking soda
1/2 tsp. salt
1/2 cup finely chopped walnuts
1/3 cup light oil, sunflower or safflower
1 large egg
1 8-ounce can crushed pineapple, juice packed
1/2 cup golden raisins

1. Prepare 8 1/2 x 4 x 2 1/2 inch loaf pan (or 9 x 5 x 3 inch) with oil or lecithin/oil. Set aside.
2. Finely grate zucchini. Let it drain while you combine the dry ingredients.
3. Preheat oven to 350 degrees.
4. In a large bowl, mix together flours, dry milk powder, baking soda, salt and finely chopped nuts. Set aside.
5. In blender, combine oil, egg, crushed pineapple and juice, and raisins. Puree on high speed.
6. Add blended pineapple mixture to dry ingredients. Mix to moisten evenly.
7. Squeeze out zucchini. It should equal 1/2 cup packed. Stir grated zucchini into batter until evenly distributed.
8. Turn batter into prepared pan and smooth it out with a rubber scraper.
9. Bake at 350 degrees for 70 minutes or until browned and inserted cake tester comes out clean.
10. Remove bread from pan, tipping it on its side to cool to room temperature.
11. Wrap and refrigerate.
12. This bread freezes well.

Nutritional information per serving, 90 calories, 1 fruit, 1/3 meat (high fat), 1/3 fat exchanges.

California Fruit Bread

Preparation time	30 minutes to prepare, 60 minutes to bake
Yield	1 loaf or 24 servings

Ingredients

2 cups whole wheat flour
2 T. nonfat dry milk powder
   or 2 T. soy flour (for milk free diets)
2 T. lowfat soy flour
2 tsp. baking powder
1/2 tsp. baking soda
1/4 tsp. salt
1/2 cup chopped toasted sunflower kernels
1/3 cup light oil (sunflower or safflower)
1 large egg
2 small (7 3/4 inch) very ripe bananas
1 8-ounce can crushed pineapple, juice packed
1/2 cup finely chopped, pitted dried apricots
1/2 T. grated orange peel
1/2 cup golden raisins

1. Prepare an 8 1/2 x 4 1/2 x 2 1/2 inch (or 9 x 5 x 3 inch) loaf pan with oil or lecithin/oil. Set aside.
2. Open pineapple and drain off juice. Stir it a few times so that it will drain well. Set aside. (Drink the juice, if you like.)
3. Mix together in a large bowl flours, milk powder, baking powder, baking soda, salt and sunflower kernels. Set aside.
4. In blender, process oil, egg and bananas until liquid.
5. Add banana mixture to dry ingredients.
6. Stir in drained crushed pineapple (1/2 cup), finely chopped apricots, grated orange peel and raisins.
7. Turn batter into prepared loaf pan and distribute evenly.
8. Bake at 350 degrees for 60 minutes or until golden and tests done.
9. Remove loaf from pan, and rest on a board on its side until completely cooled.
10. Refrigerate wrapped.
11. This bread freezes well.

Nutritional information   per slice (1/24), 110 calories, 1 bread, 1 fat exchange

Baking Tips for Muffins

1. For optimal rising, preheat oven and prepare pans. Once the leavening agent (baking soda, baking powder) is moistened, it goes to work, so the shorter the amount of time between moistening the leavening and baking the muffins, the lighter your muffins.
2. If you use cupcake pans your muffins will be larger than those calculated here and your yield will be fewer muffins per recipe. If you wish to match the indicated yield, simply put less batter into each cup and gauge the baking time accordingly. They should not take as long to bake and will be somewhat flatter and wider than mine.
3. Any of these muffins can be baked at a lower temperature (350-375 degrees) if you wish to share the oven with something else. Just allow the muffins longer baking time.

Apricot Bran Muffins

Preparation time 30 minutes to prepare and bake
Yield 16 golden muffins

Ingredients
1 1/2 cup whole wheat flour
1/2 cup bran
1 tsp. baking soda
1/2 tsp. cinnamon
1/2 tsp. allspice
1/4 tsp. salt
1 16-ounce can water packed apricots
1 large egg
1/4 cup oil
1/3 cup packed, chopped, dried apricots (about 12 halves)

1. Prepare muffin cups with oil or lecithin/oil.
2. Preheat oven to 425 degrees (F).
3. In a large bowl fork stir flour, bran, baking soda, cinnamon, allspice and salt to combine. Set aside.
4. Drain water packed apricots. (Drink or discard the juice.)
5. Blend the drained apricots on low speed of blender.
6. Add egg and oil to blended apricots and blend again, on high speed.
7. Stir blender mixture into dry ingredients, mixing to moisten.
8. Stir in chopped dried apricots until evenly distributed.
9. Fill muffin cups 2/3 full.
10. Bake at 425 degrees for 15 minutes or until golden and muffins test done.
11. Serve warm or cold.
12. These freeze well.

Nutritional information per muffin, 94 calories or 1 bread and 1/2 fat exchange

Blueberry Muffins

Preparation time 45 minutes, includes baking
Yield 15 muffins

Ingredients

 2 cups whole wheat flour
 1/2 tsp. cinnamon
 1/2 tsp. baking soda
 1/2 tsp. salt
 2 large eggs
 1 cup Applesauce (see page 25)
  or commercial unsweetened applesauce
 1/4 cup sunflower or safflower oil
 1 cup fresh or frozen (without sugar) blueberries

1. Prepare muffin cups with oil or lecithin/oil.
2. Preheat oven to 425 degrees (F).
3. In a large bowl, stir together flour, cinnamon, baking soda, and salt. Set aside.
4. In a small bowl beat eggs until lemony; then stir in applesauce and oil.
5. Pour egg mixture into the dry ingredients and beat until well mixed.
6. Gently stir in blueberries.
7. Fill prepared muffin cups 2/3 full.
8. Bake at 425 degrees for 30 minutes or until nicely browned.
9. Serve warm or cold.
10. These freeze well.

Nutritional information per muffin, 110 calories, or 1 bread and 1 fat exchange

Orange Muffins

Preparation time 30 minutes, includes baking
Yield 15 scrumptious muffins

Ingredients
1 1/2 cups whole wheat flour
2 T. lowfat soy flour
1 tsp. baking soda
1/2 tsp. cinnamon
pinch cloves
1/4 tsp. salt
2 T. freshly grated orange rind (1 medium orange)
1/2 cup raisins
3/4 cup orange juice, unsweetened
2 large eggs
1/4 cup oil

1. Prepare muffin cups with oil or lecithin/oil.
2. Preheat oven to 425 degrees (F).
3. In a large bowl combine flours, baking soda, cinnamon, cloves, salt, orange rind and raisins. Stir with a fork until mixture is uniform. Set aside.
4. In a small bowl beat 2 eggs; then beat in orange juice and oil.
5. Pour orange juice mixture into dry ingredients. Stir just until batter is evenly moistened.
6. Fill muffin cups 2/3 full.
7. Bake at 425 degrees for 15 minutes. A toothpick inserted in middle of muffin should come out clean.
8. Serve warm or cold.
9. These freeze well.

Nutritional information per muffin, 109 calories or 1 bread and 1 fat exchange

Raisin-Nut Muffins

Preparation time 45 minutes, includes baking time
Yield 15 large muffins

Ingredients

1 3/4 cups whole wheat flour
2 tsp. baking powder
1/2 tsp. cinnamon
1/2 tsp. salt
pinch allspice
1 cup Sweet Milk (see page 28)
2 large eggs
1/4 cup sunflower or safflower oil
1 cup raisins
1/2 cup chopped almonds

1. Prepare muffin cups with oil or lecithin/oil.
2. Preheat oven to 425 degrees (F).
3. In a large bowl stir together flour, baking powder, cinnamon, salt and allspice.
4. Add raisins and nuts and stir again. Set aside.
5. In a small bowl, beat eggs until lemony; then beat in sweet milk and oil.
6. Pour egg mixture into dry ingredients. Mix well.
7. Fill prepared muffin cups 3/4 full and bake at 425 degrees for 25-30 minutes or until golden and inserted toothpick comes out clean.
8. Serve warm or cold.
9. These freeze well.

Nutritional information per muffin, 155 calories or 1 bread, 1 fat and 1 fruit exchange

CHAPTER FOUR
Cakes

Birthdays and weddings seem to need the presence of a cake. Many nutrition-conscious people find themselves faced with a minor dilemma at such times: they are caught between the predominant sugar-equals-love philosophy and their own enlightened attitude, I-love-you-so-I-don't-serve-that-stuff. Hopefully, the following recipes will provide some acceptable alternatives.

My cakes use primarily whole wheat flour and are, therefore, quite filling. The lighter textured cakes such as Tut's Carob Cake, Carrot Cake and Cherry Spice Cake make excellent special occasion cakes as they are closer in texture to what most people conceptualize when they think of cake. The cakes referred to as bars are of a coarser texture and heavier crumb.

Most of these cakes can be baked ahead and frozen for 6-8 weeks, if well wrapped. However, prolonged freezing will dry them out.

Now, what about icing? Please don't. If you feel the urge to decorate, use your imagination and garnish with a few strategically placed strawberries, cherries, a thin wedge of cheese, a well-centered walnut or even a fresh violet. If you must use icing try a yogurt-cheese based icing (see page 30) and spread thinly.

Applesauce-Raisin Cake

Preparation time   1 hour to prepare and bake
Yield   One 9 x 13-inch cake, 24 servings

Ingredients

1 3/4 cups whole wheat flour
1/4 cup lowfat soy flour
1 T. baking powder
1 tsp. baking soda
1/2 tsp. salt
1/2 tsp. cloves
1/2 tsp. nutmeg
2 tsp. cinnamon
1 cup Sweet Milk (see page 28)
1/4 cup (10) packed dates
3 large eggs
1/3 cup sunflower or safflower oil
1 cup Applesauce (see page 25) or commercial
   natural style applesauce
1/2 cup chopped nuts or sunflower seeds
1 cup raisins

1. Prepare a 9 x 13-inch pan with oil or lecithin/oil.
2. Preheat oven to 375 degrees.
3. In a large bowl combine flours, baking powder, baking soda, salt, cloves, nutmeg and cinnamon. Stir with a fork, then form a well and set aside.
4. In a blender, process 1 cup Sweet Milk, dates, eggs, oil and applesauce, until mixture is smooth and uniform.
5. Pour liquid ingredients into well of dry ingredients. Mix with a spoon until all ingredients are moistened.
6. Stir in 1/2 cup chopped nuts/seeds and 1 cup raisins until evenly distributed.
7. Pour batter into prepared pan and bake at 375 degrees for 40-45 minutes.
8. When inserted toothpick or cake tester comes out clean, cake is done. Remove it from oven to cool at room temperature.
9. When cool, cut into 24 pieces, cover and refrigerate.
10. Best when served cold. This cake also freezes well.

Nutritional information   per serving, 119 calories or 1 bread and 1 fat exchange

Apricot Cheesecake

Preparation time	90 minutes. Chill several hours or overnight.
Yield	1 deep 10-inch cake. Serves 12.

Ingredients
Filling

1 cup dried apricots
1/2 cup orange juice, unsweetened
1 cup lowfat (2%) cottage cheese
1 cup Nonfat Yogurt (see page 29)
4 large eggs
1 T. unsweetened coconut
1 tsp. freshly grated orange rind
1/8 tsp. salt
2 T. whole wheat flour

Crust

1/2 cup wheat germ
1/2 cup whole wheat flour
1/2 tsp. cinnamon
1/4 cup light oil (safflower or sunflower)
1 tsp. freshly grated orange rind

Topping

1/2 cup Nonfat Yogurt (see page 29)
1 T. unsweetened coconut

1. To prepare filling: combine apricots and orange juice in a saucepan and bring them to a boil over high heat.
2. Reduce heat to low, cover and simmer 5 minutes.
3. While apricots are simmering, into the blender measure 1 cup cottage cheese and 1 cup yogurt and process until smooth.
4. Blend in one egg at a time, and set blended mixture aside.
5. Remove apricots from heat, uncover and let cool.
6. To prepare crust: in a medium bowl mix wheat germ, flour and orange rind with a fork. Add oil, stirring to moisten all ingredients evenly. Pat evenly into a deep 10-inch pie pan or a flan pan, over bottom and up sides. Set aside.
7. Preheat oven to 350 degrees.
8. Add the cooled cooked apricots and orange juice to the blended cottage cheese mixture and process until smooth.
9. Fold in orange peel, salt and 2 T. whole wheat flour.
10. Pour blended apricot mixture into the crust and bake at 350 degrees for 35 minutes. Meanwhile, prepare the topping.
11. To prepare topping: combine yogurt with coconut.
12. After cheesecake has baked for 35 minutes, spread the yogurt topping over it evenly. Bake 10 minutes at 350 degrees.
13. Allow cheesecake to cool to room temperature, cover and refrigerate several hours or overnight.
14. Slice into 12 wedges and serve cold.

Nutritional information   per serving, 172 calories, 1 fruit, 1/2 meat (medium fat), 1/2 whole milk exchange

Cherry Spice Cake

I make this frequently for birthdays.

Preparation time 1 1/2 hours to prepare and bake

Yield Twelve 2 x 2 2/3-inch servings or one 8-inch square cake

Ingredients

1 16-ounce can waterpacked sour cherries
1/2 cup Sweet Milk (see page 28)
1/2 cup packed dates
1/4 cup light oil, sunflower or safflower
2 large eggs, separated
3/4 cup Applesauce (see page 25)
   or commercial unsweetened applesauce
1 3/4 cups whole wheat flour
2 T. lowfat soy flour
2 T. nonfat dry milk powder
   or 2 T. lowfat soy flour (for milk free diets)
1 T. cinnamon
1 T. baking powder
1 tsp. baking soda
1/2 tsp. cloves
1/2 tsp. nutmeg
1/4 tsp. salt

1. Prepare an 8-inch square cake pan with oil or lecithin/oil.
2. Preheat oven to 350 degrees.
3. Drain waterpacked cherries.
4. After cherries have drained well, measure 1 cup of them and set aside.
5. In blender puree together 1/2 cup Sweet Milk with 1/2 cup packed dates.
6. Blend oil, egg yolks and natural style applesauce. Set aside next to cherries.
7. In a small bowl beat 2 egg whites until stiff and set aside next to blended ingredients and chopped cherries.
8. In a large bowl combine flours, dry milk, baking powder, baking soda, salt and spices. Stir well.
9. Gradually mix blended liquid ingredients into dry ingredients until well moistened.
10. Gently stir in cherries.
11. Then fold in the egg whites just until combined.
12. Pour batter into the prepared cake pan and bake at 350 degrees for 50 minutes.
13. Cool cake to room temperature.
14. Cut and serve. Refrigerate covered.

Variation Substitute 1 cup fresh sliced strawberries for cherries.

Nutritional information per serving, 160 calories or 1 bread, 1 fruit and 1 fat exchange

Tut's Carob Cake

The best of the best, this cake's a treasure.

Preparation time — 75 minutes to prepare and bake

Yield — One 8-inch square cake or sixteen 2 x 2-inch servings

Ingredients

1 3/4 cups whole wheat flour
2 T. lowfat soy flour
2 T. nonfat dry milk powder
   or 2 T. soy flour (for milk free diets)
2 tsp. baking powder
1/2 tsp. baking soda
1/4 tsp. salt
1 1/2 cups Applesauce (see page 25)
   or commercial natural style applesauce
1/3 cup light oil, sunflower or safflower
1 large egg
1/2 cup packed pitted dates
1 tsp. cinnamon
1/2 tsp. cloves
1/2 tsp. nutmeg
1 tsp. freshly grated orange rind
2 T. carob powder

1. Prepare an 8-inch square or 9-inch round cake pan with oil or lecithin/oil. Set aside.
2. Preheat oven to 350 degrees (F).
3. In a large bowl, combine flours, nonfat dry milk powder, baking powder, baking soda and salt. Stir, then set aside.
4. Into the blender put applesauce, oil, egg, dates, spices, orange rind and carob powder. Process until dates are very finely chopped.
5. Stir blended carob mixture into dry ingredients, mixing just until batter is consistent in appearance.
6. Pour batter into prepared pan and bake at 350 degrees for 45 minutes or until inserted cake tester comes out clean.
7. Cool to room temperature, cover and refrigerate. Serve cold.
8. This cake freezes well.

Nutritional information — per 2 x 2-inch serving, 120 calories, 1 fruit, 1/2 fat, 1/3 meat (high fat) exchange

Carrot Cake

Preparation time 30 minutes to prepare, 45-50 to bake
Yield 8-inch square cake or 16 2 x 2-inch pieces

Ingredients
3 large carrots
1 large egg
3/8 cup light oil, sunflower or safflower
1 8-ounce can crushed pineapple, packed in own juice
1 cup raisins
1 tsp. vanilla extract
1 1/2 cups whole wheat flour
1 tsp. cinnamon
1/4 tsp. nutmeg
1/4 tsp. allspice
1/2 tsp. salt
1 1/2 tsp. baking powder

1. Scrub and grate the carrots. Measure 1 cup and set aside.
2. Prepare an 8 x 8-inch square baking pan with lecithin/oil.
3. In a blender combine egg, oil, crushed pineapple and juice, raisins and vanilla. Process until raisins are finely chopped.
4. Measure flour, spices, salt and baking powder into a large mixing bowl. Stir well.
5. Add blended mixture and grated carrots to dry ingredients, mixing until batter is uniform.
6. Spread batter into an oiled pan and bake at 350 degrees for 45-50 minutes or until inserted cake tester comes out clean.
7. Cool.
8. Refrigerate.
9. This cake can be frozen, then thawed in the refrigerator for later use.

Nutritional information per serving, 130 calories or 1 bread and 1 fat exchange

Grandma's Fruit Cake

My grandma made this fruitcake with wine and soaked it in
brandy, dousing it daily, for at least 30 days before serving it.
Obviously, mine is a more temperate version. It is very sweet so
you will want to slice it as thinly as possible and then halve those
pieces. For easy slicing, chill the cake thoroughly and keep it
tightly wrapped in the refrigerator to avoid drying out and crumb-
ling.

Preparation time   30 minutes to prepare, 2 hours to bake
Yield   One 9 x 5 x 3-inch loaf or 36 slices

Ingredients
2 cups packed raisins
3 cups packed chopped mixed dried fruit (peaches, apples,
    apricots, prunes, figs)
2 cups chopped walnuts
1 1/4 cup whole wheat flour
2 T. lowfat soy flour
2 T. nonfat dry milk powder
    or 2 T. soy flour (for milk free diets)
1/4 cup strong decaffinated coffee
1/2 cup unsweetened purple grape juice
1/3 cup pitted, packed dates
2 large eggs
1/3 cup light oil (sunflower or safflower)

1. Chop the dried fruit and nuts and place them in a large bowl.
2. Add flours and dry milk and stir to mix. Set aside.
3. In blender pour coffee and grape juice; add dates, eggs and
   oil. Process until liquid and uniformly smooth. Set aside.
4. Preheat oven to 300 degrees, moving rack to the lowest shelf.
5. Prepare a 9 x 5 x 3 inch loaf pan with oil or lecithin/oil.
6. Stir blender mixture into fruit and flour in large bowl. Mix
   until all ingredients are moistened.
7. Turn batter into loaf pan pressing it down to eliminate any air
   pockets. Poke through the batter every few inches with a fork
   to force the batter down. It's important that the batter is
   packed down solid for successful slicing later.
8. Bake on lowest oven shelf at 300 degrees for 2 hours or until
   evenly browned and inserted cake tester comes out clean.
9. Turn cake out of pan and rest it on its side to cool to room
   temperature.
10. Wrap tightly and refrigerate until thoroughly chilled before
    slicing.

Nutritional information   per slice (1/2 x 2 1/2 x 1/2-inches), 146 calories, 1 fruit, 1 fat,
2/3 bread, 1/3 meat (lean) exchanges

Gingerbread

Preparation time 1 hour to prepare and bake

Yield One 8 x 8 inch cake or sixteen 2 x 2 inch pieces

Ingredients
1 3/4 cups whole wheat flour
1/4 cup lowfat soy flour
1/4 cup buckwheat flour
1 T. cinnamon
1 T. ginger
1 T. baking powder
1 tsp. baking soda
1/4 tsp. salt
1/4 tsp. cloves
1 1/2 cups Sweet Milk (see page 28)
2 large eggs
1/4 cup light oil, safflower or sunflower
1/3 cup packed pitted dates
1/3 cup raisins

1. Prepare an 8 x 8-inch pan with oil and
1. Prepare an 8 x 8-inch cake pan with oil or lecithin/oil. Set aside.
2. Preheat oven to 350 degrees.
3. In a large bowl, fork stir to combine flours, spices, baking powder, soda and salt. Set aside.
4. Process remaining ingredients in the blender until mixture is uniform and fruit is finely chopped.
5. Pour blender mixture into dry ingredients. Beat to moisten.
6. Pour batter into prepared pan.
7. Bake at 350 degrees for 45-50 minutes or until golden and edges are dry. Insert a toothpick in the center of the cake. It should come out clean.
8. Cool to room temperature.
9. Refrigerate, tightly wrapped.
10. This can be frozen.

Nutritional information per 2 x 2-inch piece, 90 calories or 1/2 bread, 1/2 milk (nonfat) 1/4 fruit exchanges

Sunshine Squares

Every winter my grandfather writes "I'm sending you some of this Florida sunshine," and ships me a case of big, beautiful oranges. This cake uses the grated rind from one of those oranges and undiluted orange juice concentrate for natural sweetness. It's especially delicious with a cup of coffee or a tall glass of milk.

Preparation time   1 hour and 10 minutes to mix and bake
Yield   One 9 x 13-inch pan or 24 squares

Ingredients
1/2 T. grated orange rind (grated rind from one orange)
1 1/2 cups whole wheat flour
1/2 cup lowfat soy flour
1/4 tsp. salt
4 tsp. baking powder
1 tsp. baking soda
2 large eggs
1 16-ounce can undiluted orange juice concentrate, at room temperature
1/3 cup safflower or sunflower oil
1 tsp. vanilla extract

1. All ingredients should be at room temperature.
2. Scrub the orange with a vegetable brush, dry it and grate until you have at least 1/2 T. orange peel. Set this grated rind aside.
3. Preheat oven to 350 degrees and prepare a 9 x 13-inch baking pan with lecithin/oil or oil.
4. In a large mixing bowl combine flours, salt, baking powder and baking soda.
5. In a medium bowl beat eggs with oil and vanilla. Then stir in orange juice concentrate and orange peel.
6. Add orange juice mixture to flour mixture and beat until well mixed.
7. Pour batter into prepared pan and bake at 350 degrees for 35-40 minutes or until inserted cake tester comes out clean.
8. Cool. Cut into 24 squares.
9. Refrigerate in an airtight container or freeze wrapped. Enjoy the sunshine!

Nutritional information   1 square, 95 calories or 1 bread and 1/2 fat exchange

Frosty Fruit Shortcake

This recipe sandwiches frozen strawberries with pineapple and bananas between layers of shortcake for an out-of-season version of an old favorite.

Preparation time	1 hour to prepare and bake
Yield	6 generous servings

Ingredients
Shortcake

(At room temperature)
1 large egg
3/4 cup skim milk
1/2 tsp. vanilla
1/4 cup Blended Butter (see page 26)
    or 2 T. light oil and 2 T. butter
1 cup plus 2 T. whole wheat flour
3/4 tsp. baking powder
1/4 tsp. baking soda
1/4 tsp. salt

Fruit Filling

1 20-ounce can, juice packed, pineapple chunks
2 cups frozen strawberries, unsweetened
1 small (7 3/4-inch) ripe banana
6 T. Nonfat Vanilla Yogurt (see page 131)
    or commercial lowfat vanilla yogurt

1. Prepare a small (8 1/2 x 4 1/2 x 2 1/2-inch) loaf pan with oil or lecithin/oil and set aside.
2. Preheat oven to 350 degrees (F).
3. Separate the egg, putting the white in a mixer bowl and the yolk in a small bowl. Whip the egg white until stiff, then set aside.
4. Beat egg yolk, then add vanilla and milk, beating until combined. Set the mixture aside.
5. In a large bowl, fork stir flour, baking powder, baking soda and salt.
6. Cut in Blended Butter or oil and butter until mixture is coarse.
7. Stir in the milk mixture, and beat until all ingredients are moistened.
8. Fold in the stiffly beaten egg whites.
9. Turn batter into prepared pan, spreading it evenly with a spatula or the back of a spoon.
10. Bake at 350 degrees for 40 minutes or until golden and inserted cake tester comes out clean.
11. While cake bakes, drain pineapple chunks, slice bananas and slice frozen strawberries if they are whole.

12. Combine fruit in a medium-sized bowl and cover.
13. When cake is done baking, let it cool 10 minutes, then remove it from the pan. Let it cool to room temperature.
14. Cut cooled cake into 12 slices.
15. Place one slice of cake on each serving plate.
16. Then spoon some fruit over it, top this with another slice of cake, 1 T. of vanilla yogurt and more fruit.
17. Serve immediately.

Nutritional information   per serving (1/6), 248 calories or 1 fruit, 1 bread, 1 fat and 1/2 milk (whole) exchanges

Variations

Fresh Strawberry Shortcake   Substitute 4 cups sliced fresh strawberries for pineapple, bananas and frozen strawberries. Proceed as recipe directs.

Nutritional information   per serving (1/6), 218 calories, 1 bread, 1 fat, 1/2 fruit and 1/2 milk (whole) exchange

Peach Shortcake   Use 4 cups sliced fresh or frozen (without sugar of course!) peaches in place of pineapple, bananas and frozen strawberries. Proceed as recipe directs.

Nutritional information   per serving (1/6), 224 calories, 1 bread, 1 fat, 3/4 fruit and 1/2 milk (whole) exchange

Blueberry Shortcake   Use 4 cups fresh or frozen (unsweetened) blueberries in place of pineapple, bananas and frozen strawberries. Proceed as recipe directs.

Nutritional information   per serving (1/6), 241 calories, 1 fruit, 1 bread, 1 fat and 1/2 milk (whole) exchange

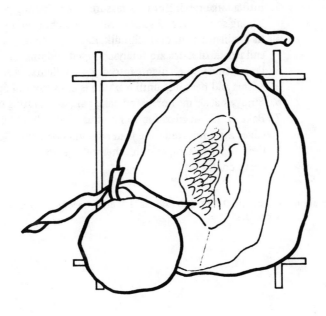

Pumpkin Bars

If you would like to bake a pumpkin, see Pumpkin Pie (page 109) for instructions.

Preparation time 60 minutes
Yield One 9 x 13-inch pan or 15 servings

Ingredients
1 3/4 cup whole wheat flour
1/4 cup, lowfat soy flour
1 T. baking powder
1 tsp. baking soda
1/2 tsp. salt
1 T. cinnamon
1/2 tsp. cloves
1/2 tsp. nutmeg
1/4 tsp. ginger
1/3 cup light oil (safflower or sunflower)
1/4 cup nonfat milk (skim)
1/3 cup pitted, packed dates
3/4 cup pumpkin, fresh or canned
3/4 cup Applesauce (see page 25)
    or commercial natural style applesauce
1 large egg
1/2 cup chopped walnuts
1 cup raisins

1. Prepare a 9 x 13-inch cake pan with oil or lecithin/oil. Set aside.
2. Preheat oven to 350 degrees (F).
3. Into a large mixing bowl, measure flours, baking powder, baking soda, salt and spices. Stir to combine and set aside.
4. In the blender process oil, milk, dates, pumpkin, applesauce and egg until dates are finely chopped and mixture is smooth.
5. Pour blended ingredients into dry ingredients. Add nuts and raisins and beat just until mixture is consistent in appearance.
6. Empty batter into prepared cake pan, distributing evenly.
7. Bake at 350 degrees for 40 minutes. Cake should be golden, edges dry. Inserted cake tester should come out clean.
8. Cool to room temperature, then refrigerate.
9. Serve cold.

Nutritional information per serving (1/15), 180 calories, 1/2 meat (medium fat), 1 fat, 2 fruit exchanges

Blueberry Crumpet

Preparation time   25 minutes to prepare, 1 hour to bake
Yield   1 1/2 quarts, serves 9

Ingredients
1 cup whole wheat flour
1 T. lowfat soy flour
1 tsp. baking powder
1/2 tsp. nutmeg
1/4 tsp. salt
2 T. butter, room temperature
2 T. light oil, safflower or sunflower
1 large egg, lightly beaten
3/8 cup Sweet Milk (see page 28)
    or 3/8 cup unsweetened apple juice
2 cups fresh blueberries, or frozen, without sugar

1. Prepare a 1 1/2 quart casserole dish with oil or lecithin/oil.
2. Preheat oven to 350 degrees (F).
3. In a large bowl, fork stir to combine flours, baking powder, nutmeg and salt.
4. Cut butter into dry ingredients.
5. Mix in oil, beaten egg and Sweet Milk.
6. Spread this batter into the prepared casserole dish.
7. Top with blueberries, spreading them evenly.
8. Bake, uncovered, for 1 hour or until batter is done and berries are bubbly hot.
9. Serve warm or cold, plain or with a dollop of nonfat yogurt.
10. Refrigerate extras, covered.

Nutritional information   per serving, 127 calories or 1 bread and 1 fat exchange

Puff Pancake Dessert

This crusty, golden, saucer-shaped popover is a delicious vehicle for yogurt and fruit.

Preparation time	15 minutes to prepare, 20 minutes to bake.
Yield	8 servings

Ingredients

2 T. Blended Butter (see page 26) or 1 T. butter and 1 T. oil
3 large eggs, separated
1/2 cup skim milk
1/2 cup finely ground whole wheat flour
1 1/2 cups fresh or frozen (without sugar) berries or peaches
1/2 cup Nonfat Yogurt (see page 29)
1/2 tsp. vanilla extract

1. Set oven rack in lowest position and preheat oven to 450 degrees (F).
2. In a small saucepan, over low heat, melt Blender Butter, set aside.
3. Very lightly oil the bottom and sides of a nine inch cast iron skillet or other heavy skillet with an oven proof handle. Heat the oiled skillet in the oven while you prepare the batter; you want it to get very hot.
4. In a medium bowl beat egg yolks until lemony, then whisk in skim milk and flour, beating until smooth.
5. Whisk in the cooled melted Blender Butter. Set batter aside.
6. Beat egg whites until stiff peaks form. Fold egg whites into batter mixture.
7. Pour mixture into the hot skillet, distributing evenly by tilting the pan in a circular motion. Batter should run up the edges of the pan and cling there. Work quickly to retain heat.
8. Bake on bottom oven rack for 15 minutes at 450 degrees, then lower heat to 350 degrees and bake for another 5 minutes until dark brown and custardy interior is dry and set. (Insert a toothpick to test, if you wish.)
9. Combine yogurt with vanilla and spread evenly over the warm popover. Fill with sliced strawberries, peaches or other fruit.
10. Serve immediately, rolled and sliced, or cut into wedges.
11. This makes a lovely dessert or a very special breakfast.

Nutritional information 1/8 of recipe, 110 calories, 1/2 (whole) milk exchange, 1/2 fruit exchange

CHAPTER FIVE
Cookies

When I was in fourth grade, my mom was my homeroom mother, responsible for classroom party refreshments. I come from a large family so her volunteering to do extra cooking was very generous.

I remember fondly the care and attention she put forth on those occasions—especially for the Halloween party. After we decided on cutout cookies, we discussed which cutter shape would be just right. After some deliberation, we decided that owls would be the perfect shape. Then, on baking day, she told me that she wanted to do the cookies herself, from start to finish. It must have been her sincerity that touched me. I understood how she felt about working alone. Convinced that I was helping by being close, but not in the same room, I sat in the living room and watched the original King Kong movie on the 5 o'clock Big Show. At the commercials (and the scary parts) I would stick my head into the kitchen to see how our owls were coming along and to say something encouraging or to ask a question. They were beautiful little cookies—to the last detail. I was so proud of them and her.

Paradoxically, I don't even remember that Halloween party. I guess it was unimportant compared to my mother's earnest devotion.

Kiflis

Preparation time	20 minutes to prepare, chill several hours or overnight
Yield	18 dozen 2-inch cookies

Ingredients

2 large eggs
1 cup Nonfat Yogurt (see page 29)
   or commercial plain nonfat yogurt
1/2 cup light oil, safflower or sunflower
1/2 cup butter, room temperature
4 cups whole wheat flour
1 cup unbleached flour

1. In large mixing bowl beat well eggs, yogurt, oil and butter, (or 1 cup Blended Butter).
2. Add 3 cups of the whole wheat flour and 1 cup unbleached flour. Mix well.
3. Knead in more (1 cup) whole wheat flour, until dough is smooth and dough can be shaped into 4 balls.
4. Flatten dough and wrap securely.
5. Freeze for future use or refrigerate several hours or overnight.
6. Later in day or next day have filling ready. See Cookie Fillings (page 65).
7. To shape Kiflis, on a lightly floured surface roll dough 1/8-inch thick. With pastry wheel or cookie cutter, cut 2-inch squares. Place 1/2 tsp. filling in each cookie and bring up 2 opposite corners, overlapping and pinching to seal.
8. Place on ungreased cookie sheets and bake at 400 degrees for 8-12 minutes (when edges are golden).
9. Remove and cool. Store in airtight container in refrigerator or freezer.

Other Shapes for Filled Cookies

Barbara's Stars

My sister cuts out the dough with a star-shaped cutter, puts filling in the center, then brings the points together pinching with ice water to seal. Neat, eh?

Yield   9 dozen from half of dough

Envelopes

Roll dough 1/8-inch thick. Cut into a diamond or square shape. Spread with filling then fold over each point.

Yield   9 dozen from half of dough

Pinwheels   Roll dough 1/8-inch thick. Cut into 2 or 3-inch squares with a sharp knife, slit into each corner about 1 inch. Put 1/2 tsp. of filling in center of each cookie then turn in every other "half corner."

Yield   7-8 dozen from half of dough

Sandwich Cookies   Roll dough 1/8-inch thick. Cut into desired shapes—hearts, bells, stars, circles, etc. Cut two identical shapes for each cookie. Cut circle from one shape—use a small round cutter or bottle top. Put filling on whole cookie (that has a center). Top with cookie from which the center has been cut—pinch sides to seal with ice water.

Yield   8 dozen from entire dough recipe

Jackie's Roll-ups   Roll 1/4 of dough out to a rectangle, 1/8-1/4 inch thick. Spread with an even layer of filling. Gently roll up jelly roll fashion, pinching edge to seal. Using a very sharp knife, slice cookies 1/4-inch thick.

Yield   10-11 dozen from entire dough recipe

Fig Filling

Ingredients   **1 cup pitted dates or figs**
1/2-3/4 cup hot water
1/2 cup finely chopped walnuts or sunflower seeds

1. Combine dates and 1/2 cup hot water in blender. Blend on high, adding more water if necessary until mixture has pasty texture.
2. Empty date puree into a small bowl and stir in finely chopped nuts.
3. Filling should be thick.

Nutritional information   per cookie, 26 calories, 1/4 bread, 1/5 fat exchange

Apricot Coconut Filling

Ingredients

1 cup dried apricots
1/3 cup hot water (add more if needed)
1/3 cup unsweetened flaked coconut

1. Combine apricots and 1/3 cup hot water in blender. Process, adding more water, a tablespoon at a time, if necessary, to make a smooth paste.
2. Empty apricot puree into a small bowl and stir in coconut. Filling should be thick.

Nutritional information   per cookie, 26 calories, 1/4 bread, 1/5 fat exchange

Prune Filling

Ingredients

20 large prunes
water
1/2 cup finely chopped walnuts

1. Put prunes in a strainer or steamer and set it in a saucepan over about 2 inches of water.
2. Bring water to a boil and steam, on low, covered for 10 minutes.
3. Remove from heat and let cool until prunes aren't too hot to handle.
4. Pit prunes, feeling for pit edge and slicing in at pit edge with a sharp paring knife, peeling fruit away from pit.
5. Place prunes in the blender and add about 1/4 cup water (you can use any water left inthe saucepan if you wish). Process on high until prunes are pureed, adding water 1 T. at a time as needed.
6. Spoon puree into a small bowl and stir in finely chopped nuts.

Nutritional information   per cookie, 26 calories, 1/4 bread, 1/5 fat exchanges

Apple Filling

Ingredients

1 cup Apple Butter (see page 24)
    or commercial unsweetened apple butter
1/2 cup finely chopped almonds

1. In a small bowl combine Apple Butter and finely chopped almonds.

Nutritional information   per cookie, 25 calories, 1/4 bread, 1/5 fat exchanges

Pineapple Filling

Ingredients

1 20-ounce can juice packed crushed pineapple
1/4 tsp. ground ginger
1/2 cup unsweetened coconut or finely chopped pecans

1. Cook crushed pineapple and juice in a saucepan over medium heat, to thicken. Stir constantly. Cook for about 20 minutes.
2. Stir in ginger. Empty mixture into the blender.
3. Process the cooked crushed pineapple in the blender.
4. Spoon pineapple puree into a small bowl and add chopped pecans or coconut, mixing well.

Nutritional information   per cookie, 26 calories, 1/4 bread, 1/5 fat exchanges

Peach Filling/Berry Filling

Ingredients

2 cups berries or peaches or a combination
1/2 cup finely chopped almonds

1. Put fruit in a medium saucepan. Cover and cook over low heat for 10 minutes.
2. Remove lid and raise heat to medium high.
3. Cook, stirring until fruit has thickened, 20-30 minutes.
4. Stir in almonds.

Nutritional information   per cookie, 24 calories, 1/4 bread, 1/5 fat exchanges

Cherry Filling

Ingredients

2 cups fresh sweet cherries, pitted
1/8 tsp. almond extract
1/2 cup finely chopped almonds

1. Prepare as for Peach Filling/Berry Filling.

Nutritional information   per cookie, 25 calories, 1/4 bread, 1/5 fat exchanges

Peanut Butter Raisin

Ingredients

1/2 cup natural style peanut butter
1 cup raisins, chopped
1/4 cup orange juice

1. In a small bowl beat together peanut butter and orange juice.
2. Stir in raisins, adding a little water if needed to make a smooth paste consistency of the filling.

Nutritional information   per cookie, 30 calories, 1/4 bread, 1/4 fat exchange

Chefoo's Easy Apple Puffs

Chefoo, besides being a seaport in China, is a word I coined meaning a chef's snafu. Ever had a chefoo? Yeah, me too. In fact the first time I tried out this idea, one thing after another seemed to go wrong. Now the recipe is perfect—no chefoos for you on this one!

Preparation time 1 hour (prepare kiflis dough early in day or a day in advance)
Yield 70 2 x 1 1/2-inch puffs (3 1/2 cups filling)

Ingredients

1/2 batch Kiflis Dough (see page 64)

2 packed cups (8 ounces) dried apples
1 cup hot water
1 cup raisins, chopped
2 large eggs
1/2 cup finely chopped walnuts
1 tsp. cinnamon

1. Prepare Kiflis Dough and chill it thoroughly.
2. In blender, measure dried apples; add eggs and 3/4 cups of the water and blend.
3. Stop blender and redistribute ingredients, blend again adding a tablespoon of water at a time (up to 4 T.) as needed, until mixture is fairly smooth.
4. Turn out apple mixture into a medium sized bowl, stir in chopped raisins, walnuts and cinnamon.
5. Refrigerate filling until ready to use.
6. To assemble apple puffs: on lightly floured board, roll out 1/4 of Kifli pastry 1/8-inch thick and cut to strips 4 inches wide.
7. Spoon apple filling down the length of the rectangle, on the side closest to you (see illustration), leaving a 1/2 x 2-inch border of dough.
8. Gently fold over the top 2 inches of the border using a large spatula and seal edge with the tines of a fork.

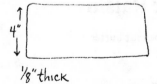
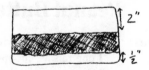

9. With a sharp knife, cut puffs 1 1/2-inches long and place on an unoiled cookie sheet.
10. Bake at 400 degrees for 8-10 minutes.
11. Repeat procedure using all dough and filling.

Variation   Chefoo's Easy Peach Puffs: Substitute dried peaches for dried apples and proceed as recipe directs.

Nutritional information   per cookie, 50 calories, 1/2 bread, 1/3 fat exchange

Apple Butter Bars

Delicious chewy bars with a granola crunch.

Preparation time   20 minutes to prepare, 35 minutes to bake
Yield   18 2 1/2 x 1 1/4-inch scrumptious bars

Ingredients
1/2 cup whole wheat flour
1/2 tsp. baking soda
2 cups Granola (see page 70)
1 large egg
1 cup Apple Butter (see page 24)
**   or commercial unsweetened apple butter**
1 tsp. vanilla

1. Prepare an 8 x 8-inch pan with oil or lecithin/oil.
2. Preheat oven to 350 degrees (F).
3. In a medium bowl, fork stir whole wheat flour and baking soda.
4. Stir in Granola. Set aside.
5. In a large bowl beat egg until lemony.
6. Beat in Apple Butter and vanilla.
7. Stir granola mixture into liquid ingredients until mixture is uniform. It should be very stiff.
8. Pat dough into prepared pan and press evenly with back of spoon or fingertips.
9. Bake at 350 degrees for 35-40 minutes or until evenly browned.
10. Cool to room temperature.
11. Cut into 18 bars. Refrigerate in airtight container or wrap individually for lunch boxes. These freeze well.

Nutritional information   1 bar (2 1/2 x 1 1/4-inch), 66 calories or 1 bread exchange

Granola

A combination of triticale, oat and wheat flakes is delicious. I like to use at least 2 cups of triticale flakes to boost the protein content.

Preparation time 20 minutes; drying time, 3 hours
Yield 11 cups

Ingredients
3/4 cup packed, pitted dates
1 cup plus 2 T. hot water
1/2 cup almonds (about 52)
1/2 cup sesame seeds
1 1/2 T. vanilla extract
1/2 T. salt
1/4 cup lowfat soy flour
1/4 cup whole wheat flour
7 cups of rolled flakes
2 cups raisins

1. In blender, combine on low then high, pitted dates and 1/2 cup hot water.
2. Then blend in almonds and another 1/2 cup plus 2 T. hot water.
3. Add and blend in on low, sesame seeds, vanilla and salt. Stop blender frequently to push ingredients on top to the bottom until mixture is uniform.
4. In a large bowl combine flours and flakes.
5. Pour the blended ingredients into the dry ingredients and with a wooden spoon combine, until mixture is crumbly and evenly moistened.
6. Spread mixture onto cookie sheets in layers about 1/2-inch thick (or it will take longer or shorter to bake).
7. Bake at 325 degrees for 25 minutes, alternating sheets (from top to bottom) after the first 15 minutes.
8. After 25 minutes turn off the oven and allow the granola to finish drying in the closed oven for another 2 or 3 hours, until dry and completely cooled.
9. Stir in 2 cups of raisins.
10. Store in an airtight container.
11. This is a delicious snack alone, or can be served with milk or yogurt.

Variation You can replace the dates and raisins with dried fruit of your choice and use cashews, walnuts or some other type of nut or seed in place of the almonds.

Nutritional information per 1/2 cup, 163 calories, 1 bread, 1 fruit, 1/2 meat (high fat) exchange

Apple Butter-Peanut Butter Cookies

The last step in making these cookies is chilling them in the refrigerator. This ripens the peanut flavor.

Preparation time 45 minutes to prepare and bake, 1 hour to chill
Yield 32 moist, peanut cookies

Ingredients
1 cup Apple Butter (see page 24)
  or commercial unsweetened apple butter
1/2 cup natural style chunky peanut butter
1 tsp. vanilla
3/4 cup nonfat powdered milk
3/4 cup whole wheat flour
1/2 tsp. salt, if peanut butter is unsalted
1/2 tsp. cinnamon, if no cinnamon has been added to the
  apple butter
1/2 cup raisins

1. Prepare cookie sheet with oil or lecithin/oil.
2. Preheat oven to 350 degrees (F).
3. In a large bowl, beat apple butter, peanut butter and vanilla. Set aside.
4. Stir together in a medium bowl, powdered milk, flour, salt (optional), cinnamon (optional) and raisins.
5. Add dry ingredients to apple butter mixture and mix well.
6. Drop by teaspoon onto prepared cookie sheet. Flatten with fork dipped in ice water, making a criss-cross pattern on top.
7. Bake at 350 degrees for 10 minutes.
8. Cool. Refrigerate until well chilled. Serve cold.
9. These freeze well.

Nutritional information per cookie, 52 calories, 1/2 milk (nonfat), 1/3 fat exchanges

Banana Drops

Soft, cake-like cookies.

Preparation time   30 minutes, including baking
Yield   25 2 1/2-inch cookies

Ingredients
- 1 cup whole wheat flour
- 2 T. lowfat soy flour
- 1/2 tsp. baking soda
- 1/2 tsp. salt
- 1/4 tsp. nutmeg
- 1/2 cup, chopped nuts or sunflower seeds
- 1 small (7 3/4-inch) very ripe banana
- 1/2 cup packed pitted dates
- 1 large egg
- 1 tsp. vanilla

1. Prepare cookie sheet with oil or lecithin/oil. Set aside.
2. Preheat oven to 350 degrees (F).
3. In a large mixing bowl, combine flours, baking soda, salt, nut-meg and nuts or seeds. Stir to mix. Set aside.
4. Mash the banana in the blender. It should equal about 1/2 cup.
5. Add dates, egg and vanilla to blender and process until dates are chopped fine and mixture is uniform.
6. Pour blended banana mixture into dry ingredients and mix well.
7. Drop cookie dough by teaspoon onto oiled cookie sheet, flatten-ing and shaping with the back of a spoon.
8. Bake at 350 degrees for 10 minutes or until inserted toothpick comes out clean.
9. Cool to room temperature. Refrigerate in an airtight container.
10. These freeze well.

Nutritional information   per cookie, 49 calories, 3/4 bread exchange

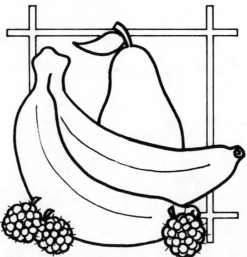

Carob Cookies

Preparation time   45 minutes to prepare and bake
Yield   20 cookies

Ingredients
    1 cup whole wheat flour
    1/2 tsp. baking powder
    1/4 tsp. salt
    1/2 tsp. cinnamon
    3/4 cup chopped walnuts
    1 cup packed pitted dates (about 40)
    2 large eggs
    1 tsp. vanilla
    3 T. carob powder

1. Preheat oven to 350 degrees (F).
2. Prepare a cookie sheet with oil or lecithin/oil.
3. In a large bowl combine flour, baking powder, salt, cinnamon and nuts. Stir until well mixed. Set aside.
4. In a blender, combine dates, eggs and vanilla. Blend on high until dates are finely chopped.
5. Add carob to blender mixture and process until carob is blended throughout and mixture is fairly smooth. There will be small date pieces in it.
6. Pour blended carob mixture into dry ingredients and stir until well mixed. Dough will be very stiff.
7. Pinch off a walnut sized piece of dough and roll it between your palms to form a ball. Shape each cookie this way, placing them about 2 inches apart on the cookie sheet, flatten with fork, criss-crossing on top.
8. Bake at 350 degrees for 8-10 minutes on next to the lowest oven rack. Cookies are done when inserted toothpick comes out clean.
9. Refrigerate in airtight container.
10. These freeze well.

Nutritional information   per cookie (1/20), 79 calories or 1 bread exchange

Cashew Halvah

Preparation time	20 minutes to prepare, 1 hour to chill
Yield	36 1 1/3 x 1 1/3-inch squares

Ingredients

1 cup sesame seeds
1 packed cup chopped raisins or currants
2/3 cup water
1/2 tsp. vanilla extract
1/8 tsp. almond extract
1/3 cup tahini
1 cup unsalted cashews, finely chopped or ground

1. Prepare an 8 x 8-inch square pan with oil or lecithin/oil. Set aside.
2. In a large saucepan, combine sesame seeds, raisins and water. Bring to a boil over high heat, and cook for 2 or 3 minutes; then stir in extracts and tahini.
3. Continue cooking and stirring for another 1 or 2 minutes. Stir in finely chopped or ground cashews.
4. Remove from heat.
5. Pat firmly and evenly into prepared pan.
6. Refrigerate at least 1 hour before cutting.
7. Cut into small squares and store in airtight container or individually wrapped.

Nutritional information   per square, 61 calories, 1/2 fruit, 1/2 fat, 1/4 meat (medium fat) exchange

Coconut Bars

Preparation time 1 hour to prepare and bake; serve cold.
Yield 20 chewy 1 3/4 x 2-inch bars

Ingredients

1 20-ounce can crushed pineapple, juice packed
1 large egg
2 cups unsweetened coconut flakes
3/4 cups whole wheat flour
1/4 cup wheat germ
1/4 tsp. salt

1. Prepare an 8 x 8-inch pan with oil or lecithin/oil.
2. Preheat oven to 350 degrees (F).
3. Drain pineapple. Measure out 3/4 cups pineapple and 3/4 cups juice for use in this recipe.
4. In a large bowl beat egg until lemony.
5. Beat in pineapple juice.
6. Stir in drained crushed pineapple and coconut; set aside.
7. In a medium bowl, fork stir flour, wheat germ and salt until
w well mixed.
8. Pour the dry ingredients into the coconut mixture and beat until all the flour is moistened.
9. Pour the batter into the prepared 8-inch square pan, patting evenly with the back of a spoon or with an impeccably clean hand.
10. Bake at 350 degrees for 45 minutes or until lightly browned and test done.
11. Cool. Cut into 20 bars. Store in an airtight container or wrap individually. Refrigerate.
12. These freeze well.

Nutritional information per serving (1/20), 91 calories, 1 fruit, 1 fat exchange

Filled Oat Bars

Preparation time	20 minutes to prepare, 35-40 minutes to bake
Yield	32 bars (2 1/4 x 1 1/2-inch)

Ingredients

1 1/2 cups packed pitted dates
1 20-ounce can crushed pineapple, juice packed
1/2 cup water
1 1/4 cups whole wheat flour
2 T. lowfat soy flour
2 T. nonfat milk powder (or additional 2 T. soy flour
   for milk free diets)
1/2 cup unsweetened coconut
1 1/2 cups uncooked oat flakes (old fashioned rolled oats)
1/2 tsp. salt
1/2 tsp. baking soda
1/4 cup light oil (sunflower, safflower)
1/4 cup butter, room temperature
2 large eggs

1. In a saucepan on high, heat dates, 1 cup of the crushed pineapple with juice and water to boiling.
2. Simmer on high until thickened, stirring constantly, breaking up dates with the spoon. This thickening will take about five minutes and the resulting mixture will be paste-like. Remove this puree from the heat and set it aside to cool.
3. Meanwhile in a large bowl, combine flours, dry milk, coconut, oat flakes, salt and baking soda. Stir to distribute all ingredients evenly.
4. Mix in softened butter and oil, eggs, and remaining pineapple and juice. Beat until well combined.
5. Preheat oven to 350 degrees (F).
6. Prepare a 9 x 13-inch baking pan with lecithin/oil or oil. Then pat half of the oatmeal batter into the pan, spreading it thinly and evenly with a rubber scraper or spatula.
7. Spoon cooled date-pineapple puree over oatmeal mixture, spreading evenly to cover the bottom oatmeal layer.
8. Finish by spreading the remaining half of the oatmeal batter over the puree, distributing it carefully and evenly.
9. Bake at 350 degrees for 35-40 minutes or until lightly browned.
10. Cool to room temperature. Cut into 32 bars (2 1/4 x 1 1/2-inch).
11. Refrigerate individually wrapped or in an airtight container.
12. These freeze well.

Nutritional information   per bar (2 1/4 x 1 1/2-inch), 102 calories, 1 bread, 2/3 fat exchange

Variation   Apricot Oat Bars: substitute 1 1/2 cups dried apricot halves for dates. Proceed as recipe directs.

Nutritional information   per bar (2 1/4 x 1 1/2-inch), 98 calories, 1 bread, 2/3 fat exchange

Empanados

Preparation time About 1 hour, depending on your choice of filling
Yield 2 1/2 dozen

Make up a recipe of your favorite 2-crust pie pastry. I use the recipe on page 105.

Roll pie pastry out thinly (1/8-1/4-inch) and cut into 3-inch (diameter) circles with a biscuit cutter.

Place circles on a cookie sheet and fill. Moisten edges with water, fold in half, pressing edges with fork to seal.

Bake at 400 degrees for 15-18 minutes. Serve warm or cold. These can be frozen.

Fillings

Pineapple 1 cup drained, crushed pineapple mixed with 1/4 cup chopped pecans or 1/4 cup grated, unsweetened coconut. (Milk Free)
Nutritional information per empanado, 70 calories, 1/2 bread, 1/2 fat exchange

Applesauce-Nut 1 1/2 cup Applesauce (see page 25), cooked over medium high heat to thicken. Stir in 1/4 cup chopped walnuts. (Milk Free)
Nutritional information per empanado, 70 calories, 1/2 bread, 1/2 fat exchange

Apple-Cheese 1 cup grated apples mixed with 1/4 cup grated cheddar cheese and a little cinnamon. These may take a little longer to bake.
Nutritional information per empanado, 68 calories, 1/2 bread, 1/2 fat exchange

Berry-Peach-Cherry 2 cups fresh or frozen (unsweetened) berries, cherries or peaches heated until thickened. Cook over medium high, stirring constantly to prevent sticking. Add desired spices (Sweet Spices, see page 22). (Milk Free)
Nutritional information per empanado, 66 calories, 1/2 bread, 1/2 fat exchange

Cheese-Raisin 1 cup lowfat cottage cheese mixed with 1/4 cup raisins or other dried chopped fruit.
Nutritional information per empanado, 70 calories, 1/2 bread, 1/2 fat exchange

Your own fruit/nut/cheese combination. Si?

Janet's Best Date Cookies

Preparation time 1 hour to prepare and bake
Yield 36 cookies

Ingredients

1 3/4 cups whole wheat flour
2 T. nonfat dry milk powder
2 T. lowfat soy flour
1 tsp. baking soda
1 tsp. salt
1/2 tsp. cinnamon
1 1/3 cups water
2 cups pitted packed dates
1/4 cup light oil
1/4 cup butter
2 large eggs
2 tsp. vanilla

1. In a large mixing bowl combine flours, dry milk, baking soda, salt and cinnamon. Stir until mixture is uniform. Set aside.
2. Put water, dates, oil and butter (or 1/2 cup Blended Butter), eggs and vanilla in blender. Process until dates are very finely chopped, redistributing ingredients periodically with a narrow rubber scraper so that large date chunks will be chopped by blender blades.
3. Add blender mixture to dry ingredients. Beat a minute or two until thoroughly mixed.
4. Drop by teaspoonsful on cookie sheet and bake at 350 degrees for 12-15 minutes. Cool.
5. Store in airtight container.
6. These freeze well.

Nutritional information per cookie, 77 calories, 1/2 bread, 1/3 fruit, 1/2 fat exchanges

Variations Milk Free Variation: substitute an additional 2 T. whole wheat flour in place of dry milk powder. Complete cookies as recipe directs.

Date-Nut Cookies: add 1 cup chopped walnuts to cookie batter, mixing well.

Nutritional information per cookie, 92 calories, 1/2 bread, 1/3 fruit, 1 fat exchange

Sticks and Stones

These sticks taste like English tea biscuits. The recipe is a good one to make with young children, as all of the measurements are complete units and the cookies don't take long to bake.

Preparation time 20 minutes to prepare, 20-25 minutes to bake

Yield 24 2 1/2 x 1 1/4-inch sticks

Ingredients
1 cup packed, pitted dates (about 40)
1 tsp. vanilla
2 large eggs
1 cup whole wheat flour
1 tsp. baking powder
1 cup coarsely chopped nuts, a combination is nice, such as almonds and sunflower seeds, or pecans and cashews, or walnuts and sesame seeds

1. Prepare an 8 x 10-inch sheet (I use half of a cookie sheet) with lecithin/oil or oil.
2. Preheat oven to 350 degrees (F).
3. Measure dates and vanilla and put them into the blender.
4. Add eggs and process until dates are chopped and mixture is uniform. This is a noisy process. Set aside.
5. In a large bowl stir together flour, baking powder, and "stones" (nuts).
6. Add blended liquid ingredients to flour mixture. Stir until well combined. It gets very stiff so you may want to mix it with your hands. (Little hands are great for this and I think they improve the flavor!)
7. Spread mixture over the baking sheet, patting it out evenly.
8. Bake at 350 degrees for 20-25 minutes, or until an inserted toothpick comes out clean.
9. Cool slightly before cutting into 24 sticks.
10. Serve when completely cooled.
11. Refrigerate wrapped or in an airtight container. These freeze well.

Nutritional information   per stick (2 1/2 x 1 1/4-inch), 71 calories, 1 bread exchange

Gingerbread People

Do these when you have lots of time to putter. I spend enormous amounts of time decorating these men and women with raisins, and even shaping and stretching the cookies into shapes representative of the friends I give them to. I add hearts, tennis racquets, dogs, bicycles, backpacks, or whatever is required to personalize these cookies.

Preparation time   2 hours
Yield   16 5 x 1/4-inch cookies

Ingredients
2 1/2 cups whole wheat flour
2 T. lowfat soy flour
2 T. nonfat dry milk powder
  or 2 T. lowfat soy flour (for milk free diets)
1 tsp. ginger, ground
1/2 tsp. cinnamon
1/2 tsp. nutmeg
1/2 tsp. salt
1/8 tsp. allspice
2 large eggs
1/4 cup light oil, safflower or sunflower
1/2 cup butter, room temperature
1 cup pitted, packed dates
1 tsp. vanilla
1/4 cup raisins for decorating

1. Combine in a large bowl flours, milk powder, baking soda, spices and salt. Stir to mix. Set aside.
2. Puree in blender, eggs, oil, butter, dates and vanilla. Stop blender after about 1 minute, redistribute ingredients with narrow rubber scraper and blend again. Repeat this procedure 2 or 3 times until mixture is liquid and uniformly caramel colored.
3. Add liquid ingredients to dry mixture and beat until color is even and dough is stiff. Knead by hand if too stiff for mixer.
4. Divide dough in half. Roll out half of dough on lightly floured bread board. Roll to 1/4-inch thickness. Cut into desired shapes using cookie cutters or a sharp knife (free lance). Decorate with raisins (some ideas follow).
5. Bake on an unprepared baking sheet at 350 degrees for 8-10 minutes.
6. Cool and remove carefully to airtight container.
7. Store cookies in refrigerator.
8. Cookies and dough both freeze well.

Nutritional information   per cookie (5 x 1/4-inch), 195 calories, 1 1/2 fruit, 1 fat, 1/2 milk (whole milk)

Raisins raison d'etre   Or not only do raisins taste good—they can jazz up a cookie, too!

1. For hair, cuffs, belts, bicycle spokes, mouths . . . thinly slice raisins and lay end-to-end. Push raisins in firmly.

2. For hearts—cut into the raisin 3/4 of the length, pull raisin apart gently, push raisins into cookie firmly.

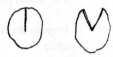

3. For smaller features such as eyes, nose, buttons—yes, and even navels—quarter raisins and push into cookies firmly.

4. For designs, patterns, flowers—cut raisins in half length or width wise and arrange geometrically.

Granola Bars

Preparation time   1 hour; add time to make granola, if necessary.

Yield   8 x 8-inch pan or 16 squares

Ingredients

2 cups Granola (see page 70)
1/2 cup pitted, packed dates
1/4 cup water
1 T. tahini (or other nut butter)

1. Prepare 8 x 8-inch square pan with oil or lecithin/oil. Set aside.
2. Preheat oven to 350 degrees (F).
3. Put dates, water and tahini in blender. Blend on low, then high speed.
4. In a medium sized bowl, measure 2 cups granola. Stir blended date mixture into granola until evenly moistened.
5. Firmly pat granola batter into the prepared pan.
6. Bake at 350 degrees for 20 minutes. Remove the pan from the oven and gently slice into 16 bars. Return the pan to the oven and finish baking for another 15-18 minutes.
7. Remove from oven and carefully re-cut. Let cool completely before removing bars from pan.
8. Wrap individually and they're ready for lunches, backpacks or the cookie jar.

Nutritional information   per 2 x 2-inch square, 58 calories, 3/4 bread exchange

Raisin Drops

Preparation time   1 hour to prepare and bake
Yield   4 dozen cookies

Ingredients

1 cup Sweet Milk (see page 28)
1/3 cup packed, pitted dates
2 tsp. vanilla
1 large egg
1/3 cup light oil
1 3/4 cup old fashioned rolled oats
1 cup whole wheat flour
2 T. lowfat soy flour
2 tsp. baking powder
1/2 tsp. salt
1/2 tsp. cinnamon
pinch cloves
pinch nutmeg
1/2 cup chopped walnuts
1/2 cup raisins

1. Prepare cookie sheets with oil or lecithin/oil.
2. Combine in blender on low, then high speed, Sweet Milk, dates, vanilla, egg and oil. Blend until uniform.
3. Add oatmeal and stir with a spoon. Let this mixture sit for about 5 minutes as oats absorb moisture.
4. Meanwhile in a large mixing bowl, combine flours, baking powder, salt and spices.
5. Turn oven on to 350 degrees (F).
6. Add oat mixture to the dry ingredients in the mixing bowl. Mix well.
7. Add nuts and raisins, then mix again.
8. Drop by teaspoonsful onto prepared cookie sheets.
9. Bake at 350 degrees for 12-15 minutes, until lightly browned and toothpick inserted in center of middle cookie comes out clean.
10. Remove from pan. Cool.
11. Store in airtight container in refrigerator.
12. These freeze well.

Nutritional information   per cookie, 47 calories, 1/2 fruit, 1/2 fat exchanges

Variation   Pineapple Drops (Milk Free): use 1 15-ounce can crushed pineapple and juice (unsweetened) in place of Sweet Milk and omit raisins. Use 1/2 cup unsweetened coconut or 1/2 cup chopped pecans in place of walnuts.

Date-Peanut Clusters

The combination of milk, peanuts and whole wheat give this cookie a protein-plus.

Preparation time 30 minutes
Yield 31 clusters (1 1/2-inch in diameter)

Ingredients

1 large egg
1/4 cup natural style peanut butter
1 tsp. vanilla
1/4 cup skim milk
1 cup packed, pitted dates
1/2 cup unsalted peanuts
1/2 cup whole wheat flour
1/2 tsp. salt (use only 1/4 tsp. salt if peanut butter or peanuts are salted)

1. Preheat oven to 350 degrees (F).
2. Break egg into the blender; add peanut butter, vanilla, milk and dates. Blend.
3. Redistribute blender ingredients with a rubber scraper and blend again. Repeat this procedure until all dates are chopped.
4. Empty the blender mixture into a medium sized bowl and add peanuts, flour and salt. Beat well.
5. Drop dough by teaspoon onto an unoiled cookie sheet, making each cluster about 1 1/2-inch in diameter.
6. Bake at 350 degrees for about 10 minutes.
7. Cool to room temperature.
8. Refrigerate in an airtight container.
9. Wrapped individually, these are great hiking snacks.
10. These also freeze well.

Nutritional information per cluster (1/31 of recipe), 53 calories, 1/4 meat (high fat), 2/3 fruit exchange

Apricot Pecan Confections

Preparation time 30 minutes
Yield 26 walnut-sized balls

Ingredients
1 cup softened, chopped dried apricots
1 cup finely chopped pecans
2 T. orange juice, unsweetened

1. To soften dried apricots, place 2 inches of water in medium sized saucepan and bring it to a boil.
2. Set the apricot halves in a steamer or a strainer and place over the boiling water.
3. Cover and steam 5-10 minutes.
4. Allow apricots to cool before handling them.
5. Finely chop apricots and measure.
6. Combine chopped apricots, pecans and orange juice in a small bowl, stirring until nuts and juice are evenly distributed.
7. Spoon out about a tablespoon of the mixture and roll it between your palms to shape it into a ball.
8. Repeat this shaping process for the rest of the batch.
9. Refrigerate balls in an airtight container or on a serving plate, covered.

Nutritional information each ball contains 45 calories, 1/2 fruit and 1/2 fat exchange

Peanut Butter Carob Balls

Preparation time 1 hour
Yield 32 balls

Ingredients
1 cup natural style peanut butter, smooth or crunchy
2/3 cup packed, chopped raisins
3 T. nonfat dry milk
2 T. carob powder
pinch salt, optional
1/2 cup unsweetened coconut, optional

1. Combine all ingredients in a large bowl, except the coconut.
2. Shape into 32 balls, rolling about 1 tsp. dough between your palms for each.
3. If desired, roll the balls in coconut.
4. Refrigerate in an airtight container or individually wrapped.

Nutritional information
1 ball without coconut: 50 calories, 1/2 fruit, 1/3 meat (high fat) exchange.
1 ball with coconut: 53 calories, 1/2 fruit, 1/3 meat (high fat) exchange.

Peanut Butter Balls

Preparation time	1 hour
Yield	40 walnut-sized balls

Ingredients

1 cup raisins
1 cup natural style peanut butter
pinch of salt (if desired)
5-6 T. nonfat dry milk powder

1. Finely chop raisins and put them into a large bowl.
2. Add peanut butter (and salt if desired).
3. Stir in half of the milk powder. Knead in remaining powder, 1 tablespoon at a time, until dough does not stick to your hands.
4. Shape into 40 walnut-sized balls or roll into three logs.
5. Refrigerate, covered or tightly wrapped. Logs must be thoroughly chilled before they can be neatly sliced.
6. To freeze, wrap individually.

Variation   Milk Free Variation: use triticale or oatmeal flakes in place of dry milk.

Nutritional information   per ball, 50 calories, 1/2 fruit and 1/3 meat (high fat) exchanges

CHAPTER SIX

Crepes

I have developed my crepe recipes through many trials. Both the recipes in this chapter are higher in protein than the majority of recipes I have seen. Also they contain whole wheat flour and no sugar.

Yogurt Crepes contain equal portions of whole wheat and unbleached white flour. They are the traditional, lighter colored crepes, but they are a little heavier and a bit richer than traditional crepes.

Whole Wheat Crepes have a more robust texture than Yogurt Crepes. And the nutty flavor, due to the 100% whole wheat flour, is more pronounced. These are very filling.

The crepes come out of the pan soft and flexible for easy filling and rolling. If you prefer a crisper crepe, simply roll the unfilled crepe into a tube, lay it seam side down on a rack and dry it in the oven on low heat until the edges are brittle. Turn it once. Fill these crepes carefully with a long-handled teaspoon. Tilt the crepe and let the filling slide from end to end. If you don't care for crisp crepes, simply fill the cooked crepe by opening it flat on a serving plate. Spoon about 1/3 cup filling down the center and fold the sides over the filling. Garnish.

I use an all-purpose 7-inch stainless steel fry pan, not exclusively used for crepes, a small butter knife for loosening the edges and turning the crepes and a wok ladle that holds about 2 T. of batter. (A large spoon will do.)

To freeze, cool the crepes to room temperature. Then stack with a piece of wax paper between each crepe. Place 6 or 8 or however many crepes you will be using at one time, in a plastic bag; press out extra air around the crepes, secure the bag and freeze. Place them on a flat surface in the freezer as they are pliable and will freeze curled around anything under them. Or put the bagged crepes in a pie tin which will provide flat even support.

To thaw, remove from freezer and thaw in the refrigerator a day ahead. Or you may thaw the crepes at room temperature a few hours before using them. I have pried apart frozen crepes, gently removed the wax paper, laid them on a baking sheet, covered the sheet with foil and thawed them in a warm oven. Be careful not to overheat the crepes. They could dry out and be difficult to roll.

The fillings I give here are prepared to my taste. You may prefer thicker, thinner or spicier fillings.

Yogurt Crepes

Preparation time	45 minutes
Yield	16-18 servings

Ingredients	**2 T. butter**
	2 T. oil
	1/2 cup whole wheat flour
	1/2 cup unbleached flour
	1/4 tsp. salt
	1/8 tsp. nutmeg
	4 large eggs
	1 1/4 cups Nonfat Yogurt (see page 29)
	1/2 T. oil (for the pan)

1. In a small pan, over low heat, melt butter. Add 2 T. oil.
2. Get out a large mixing bowl. Measure flours, salt and nutmeg into it and stir them together with a fork, forming a well in the center.
3. Break eggs into the well.
4. Whisk together eggs and flour until batter is lumpy and shiny.
5. Gradually add yogurt, whisking all the while.
6. Beat until batter is perfectly smooth.
7. Whisk in melted butter and oil. Set aside.
8. Heat 1/2 T. oil in a 7-inch pan over low heat for 10 minutes.
9. Raise heat to medium.
10. With a ladle or large spoon, deliver about 2 T. of the batter into the edge of the pan furthest away from the handle.
11. Tilt the pan in an even circular motion to coat the bottom evenly with batter.
12. Cook until edges dry and top has smooth beaded appearance.
13. Gently loosen crepe around edges with small spatula or thin, flexible table knife and turn to cook second side.
14. Second side will cook quickly (30-60 seconds). Invert pan over serving plate or board to remove crepe.
15. Repeat process with each crepe, stirring batter before spooning out each time.

Notes   You may want to throw away your first crepe. (My dog, Kelly, always gets this one.) It is usually loaded with oil and funny looking.

Once the pan becomes thoroughly heated, you can lower the heat to medium low.

A sense of humor is important. If you get some funny-shaped ones at first, don't be disheartened; pan swirling and crepe turning take a little practice.

Nutritional information   per crepe, 84 calories, 1/2 milk exchange (whole milk), or 1/2 milk exchange (nonfat) and 1 fat exchange

Whole Wheat Crepes

Preparation time   45 minutes
Yield   15-18 crepes

Ingredients
2 T. butter
2 T. oil
1 cup whole wheat flour
1/2 tsp. salt
4 large eggs
1-1 1/4 cups nonfat milk
1/2 T. oil (for the pan)

1. In a small pan, over low heat, melt butter. Add the 2 T. oil.
2. Get out a large mixing bowl. Measure flour and salt into the bowl and stir to combine. Form a well in the center.
3. Break four large eggs into the well.
4. Whisk together eggs and flour until batter is lumpy and shiny.
5. Gradually add milk, whisking all the while; add more milk for thinner crepes.
6. Beat until batter is uniform. It will be slightly lumpy.
7. Whisk in melted butter and 2 T. oil. Set aside.
8. Heat 1/2 T. oil in a 7-inch pan over low heat for 10 minutes.
9. Raise heat to medium.
10. With a ladle or large spoon, deliver about 2 T. of the batter to the edge of the pan furthest away from the handle.
11. Tilt the pan, swirling in an even circular motion to coat the bottom evenly with batter.
12. Cook until edges are dry and top has smooth, beaded appearance.
13. Gently loosen crepe around edges with small spatula or thin flexible table knife and turn to cook second side.
14. Second side will cook quickly (30-60 seconds). To remove crepe, invert pan over serving plate or wooden board.
15. Repeat process using all of the batter, stirring the batter each time before spooning it out.

Nutritional information   per crepe, 84 calories, 1/2 milk exchange (whole milk), or 1/2 milk exchange (nonfat) and 1 fat exchange

Almond Filling

Ingredients

1/2 cup Nonfat Yogurt (see page 29)
   or commercial nonfat yogurt
1/2 cup low fat cottage cheese (2% fat)
1/2 cup (about 50) almonds
1/2 cup raisins
1/4 tsp. cinnamon
1/8 tsp. almond extract
6 Whole Wheat Crepes (see page 89)

1. Set aside a few almonds for garnish.
2. Combine yogurt, cottage cheese, remaining almonds, raisins, cinnamon and almond extract in blender. Process until almonds are chopped.
3. Spoon 1/3 cup filling into each crepe.
4. Roll and arrange on serving platter or individual dessert plates.
5. Slice remaining almonds and arrange on rolled crepes.
6. Chill in the refrigerator until serving time or warm in the oven on low heat (200 degrees) for 10-15 minutes.

Nutritional information

per crepe, 213 calories or 1 milk exchange (whole milk) and 1 fruit exchange

Applesauce-Cheddar Filling

Ingredients

2 ounces grated cheddar cheese (1/2 cup)
2 cups Applesauce (see page 25)
   or commercial natural style applesauce
pinch cinnamon
7 Whole Wheat Crepes (see page 89)

1. Set aside 1/4 cup cheddar for garnish. Combine remaining cheddar (1/4 cup) with applesauce.
2. Spoon applesauce/cheddar into crepes, place filled crepes on an ovenproof platter.
3. Sprinkle with remaining 1/4 cup cheddar and cinnamon.
4. Heat in warm oven just until cheese begins to melt.
5. Serve immediately.

Variation

Instead of cheddar cheese, use 10 chopped walnuts and 1/4 cup raisins.

Nutritional information

per serving, 142 calories, 1 meat (high fat), 1 fruit exchange

Apricot Filling

Ingredients

1 cup lowfat cottage cheese (2% fat)
1/2 cup Quick Apricot Butter (see page 25)
1/4 tsp. cinnamon
2 T. water
2 dried apricot halves and cinnamon for garnish
4 Yogurt Crepes (see page 88)

1. Combine cottage cheese, Apricot Butter, cinnamon and water in blender.
2. Process until smooth, stopping blender periodically to redistribute ingredients with a narrow rubber scraper.
3. Spoon 1/3 cup filling into each crepe.
4. Roll crepes and arrange on a heat-proof serving platter or on individual dessert dishes.
5. Sprinkle with extra cinnamon and heat in warm oven (200 degrees) for 10-15 minutes or refrigerate to serve cold.
6. Thinly slice apricot halves and arrange slices over crepes for garnish.

Nutritional information

per filled crepe, 158 calories, 1 milk exchange (lowfat), 1/2 fruit exchange, 1/4 meat exchange (lean)

Carob-Raisin Filling

Ingredients

1 cup lowfat cottage cheese (2% fat)
2 T. water
1 tsp. vanilla
pinch salt
2 T. carob powder
1 cup raisins, set aside 18 raisins for garnish
6 Whole Wheat Crepes (see page 89)

1. Combine cottage cheese, water, vanilla, salt and carob in blender. Process until smooth, redistributing mixture with a narrow rubber spatula and blending until uniform.
2. Add raisins and blend just until raisins are mixed throughout.
3. With crepe opened on serving platter or dessert dish, spoon 1/3 cup of filling down center; gently lap sides over filling and roll seam side down on plate.
4. With the point of a sharp paring knife, slit reserved raisins 3/4 of the way up, lengthwise, pinch and open, arrange three of these on the center of each crepe; slit ends out.
5. Cover crepes with plastic wrap and refrigerate until serving time. Serve cold.

Nutritional information

per crepe, 200 calories, 1 milk exchange (lowfat), 1 3/4 fruit exchange

Berry Filling

Preparation time 45 minutes
Yield fills 8 crepes

Ingredients

2 cups fresh or frozen (without sugar) raspberries,
    strawberries or blueberries or a combination
1/2 cup unsweetened apple juice
1/4 cup tapioca
1 cup Nonfat Yogurt (see page 29)
    or commercial nonfat yogurt
pinch cinnamon
pinch nutmeg
mint sprigs, garnish
8 Whole Wheat or Yogurt Crepes (see page 89 or page 88)

1. Place fruit in saucepan, setting aside a few pieces for garnish, if desired.
2. Add apple juice and heat on low, covered, until fruit thaws or, if raw, until warm, about 10 minutes.
3. Uncover and stir in 1/4 cup tapioca.
4. Bring to a boil, stirring over medium high heat.
5. When it boils, remove from heat, stir once and cover. Let it sit for ten minutes, stirring again after five minutes.
6. Let it cool, uncovered, about 20 minutes or until it's not too hot to handle.
7. Pour the cooled berry tapioca into a mixing bowl. Whip on high speed, adding yogurt and spices.
8. Spoon 1/3 cup berry filling into each of 8 crepes. Arrange them on a platter or individual dessert plates.
9. Garnish with reserved fruit and mint sprigs if desired.
10. Refrigerate covered until serving time. Serve cold.

Nutritional information per crepe, 134 calories, 1 fruit, 1/2 milk (whole milk), exchanges

Other Fillings Pumpkin: use the filling for Pumpkin Pie (see page 109), garnish with chopped almonds

Sandcastle (see page 126): garnish with pecan halves

Berry: mix 1 1/2 cups of Vanilla Yogurt (see page 131) with 1 cup berries

Banana: slice 2 small ripe bananas. Fold these into Almond Yogurt (see page 131). Garnish with toasted almonds and a sprinkle of nutmeg.

CHAPTER SEVEN
Fruits

Serving Ideas

1. Fruit combinations are very appetizing in clear glasses and stemmed glassware or parfait glasses really add class.
2. Leave apple, peach, plum, nectarine and pear skins intact unless the fruit has been waxed or otherwise treated. The flavor and color of the fruit is greatly improved by leaving it whole. Peeling *is* recommended if you are preparing the fruit for very young children.
3. For fruit salads or fruit cocktails, combine fruits that have a similar texture, then add one fruit that is of a little different texture. For instance, to a citrus combination (oranges, grapefruit), add sliced banana. To a melon combination (watermelon, cantaloupe, honeydew), add fresh strawberries or blueberries.
4. Fruit and cheese make an elegant dessert. Arrange sliced, cubed or wedged fruit around one or more dessert cheeses on a plate. (See Cheeses, page 20.) Serve at room temperature.
5. Try serving fruit and vegetable combinations with cheese, yogurt or alone. One very interesting combination consists of green grapes (Thompson Seedless) and raw cauliflower. Serve the green grapes with a bowl of fresh firm cauliflowerlets nearby. Eat one grape, then one flowerlet—a tastebud stimulator!
6. Make a dip of lowfat cottage cheese thinned with a little skim milk and seasoned with a pinch of cinnamon or nutmeg. Serve with whole strawberries, peach or pineapple wedges and banana, apple or pear slices.
7. Another tasty dip is made by blending 1 cup of lowfat cottage cheese with 1 cup of walnuts, almonds or pecans. Thin with a little skim milk and process until smooth and serve chilled, with a colorful assortment of sliced, wedged or cubed fruit.
8. A fruit/vegetable dip for the knee-high set. Thin peanut butter with a little apple or orange juice. Spoon some of this into individual 3 ounce cups so that each child can dip from her own cup. Provide a variety of fresh bite-sized fruit and raw vegetables.
9. Slice cantaloupe or honeydew melon. Serve with yogurt or cottage cheese.
10. Alternate slices of fresh or canned pineapple with raspberries or strawberries. Top with yogurt.

Baked Apples

Preparation time   1 hour to prepare and bake
Yield   4 servings

Ingredients

4 small (2 1/2-inch in diameter) apples
2 T. chopped walnuts
3 T. chopped raisins
1 tsp. cinnamon

1. Wash and core apples, leaving skins unless they are waxed.
2. Place the apples in a baking pan or custard cups.
3. In a small bowl, combine nuts, raisins and cinnamon.
4. Stuff nut mixture into each apple—where the core isn't.
5. Cover with foil and bake at 350 degrees for 30 minutes or until tender.
6. Uncover and let cool 10 minutes or so before serving.
7. Cinnamon Yogurt (see page 131) tastes good with these. Or use milk, making sure the apples are cool enough so the milk won't curdle.

Nutritional information   per apple, 83 calories, 1 1/2 fruit, 1/2 fat exchanges

Broiled Bananas

Preparation time   15 minutes
Yield   serves 4

Ingredients

2 ripe, medium-sized bananas
2 pitted dates
1/4 cup unsweetened orange juice
1/2 tsp. almond extract
5 almonds, chopped

1. Peel bananas, cut them in half; then split each half lengthwise.
2. Arrange bananas cut side up in oiled baking dish.
3. In blender, chop dates by processing with orange juice and almond extract.
4. Pour orange juice mixture over bananas.
5. Place under broiler for 4 minutes.
6. Sprinkle almonds over bananas and return them to broiler for another 1-2 minutes or until almonds are toasted.
7. Serve immediately or chill in refrigerator first.

Nutritional information   per serving, 86 calories, 2 fruit exchanges

Glazed Pears

Preparation time 20 minutes to prepare, 1 hour to chill
Yield serves 7

Ingredients
1 1-pound can water packed pear halves (7 halves)
1/2 cup orange juice
1 T. Quick Apricot Butter (see page 25)
mint sprigs for garnish, optional

1. Drain pear halves. Set aside.
2. In a small, heavy skillet, combine juice and Apricot Butter.
3. Heat the orange juice mixture to boiling and stir.
4. Reduce heat.
5. Place pears, cut side down, in skillet; simmer, uncovered, basting often, for 15 minutes.
6. Place pear halves in individual serving dishes, spooning syrup over them.
7. Chill 1 hour or until serving time. Garnish with mint.

Nutritional information per serving (1/2 pear), 39 calories or 1 fruit exchange

Spiced Fruit

Preparation time 15 minutes to prepare, chill overnight
Yield 4 cups or 8 1/2-cup servings, fruit and juice

Ingredients
1 cup orange juice, unsweetened
2 cinnamon sticks
6 whole cloves
pinch ginger
1 1-pound can water packed pear slices
1 1-pound can water packed peach slices
2 small (2 1/4-inch in diameter) oranges

1. In a small saucepan, over low heat, heat orange juice, cinnamon sticks, cloves and ginger. Simmer five minutes.
2. Meanwhile, drain pears and peaches. Place them in a large bowl.
3. Peel oranges, cut them into bite-sized pieces and add them to the other fruit.
4. Pour simmered juice and spices over fruit.
5. Cover bowl and refrigerate overnight.
6. At serving time, remove cinnamon sticks and cloves.

Nutritional information per serving, 71 calories, 1 3/4 fruit exchange

Apple Crumble

Preparation time   1 hour to prepare and bake
Yield   1 1/2 quarts, 12 servings

Ingredients   6 medium (3 inches in diameter) apples
1/4 cup chopped raisins
6 T. whole wheat flour
1 T. lowfat soy flour
1 T. nonfat dry milk powder
   or 1 T. additional oat flakes (for milk free diets)
1/2 cup oat flakes (old fashioned rolled oats)
3/4 tsp. cinnamon
3/4 tsp. nutmeg
1/4 cup light oil (sunflower or safflower)

1. Prepare a 1 1/2-2 quart baking dish with oil or lecithin/oil. Set aside.
2. Wash, core and thinly slice apples. Arrange slices in the baking dish.
3. Sprinkle chopped raisins over sliced apples.
4. Combine remaining ingredients in a medium sized bowl, stirring to evenly distribute oil.
5. Spread crumble over fruit.
6. Bake for 30-35 minutes until apples are tender and topping is golden.
7. Delicious warm with yogurt (perfect with Cinnamon Yogurt) or milk. Also good cold. Makes a good breakfast on those nippy mornings.
8. Some may like this served with a wedge of sharp cheddar.

Nutritional information   per serving, 119 calories, 1 bread, 1 fat exchange

Apple Kuchen

Preparation time   1 1/2 hours to prepare and bake
Yield   serves 15 (13 x 9-inch pan)

Ingredients   2 cups whole wheat flour
Biscuit Crust   2 tsp. baking powder
1 tsp. baking soda
1/2 tsp. salt
1/4 cup light oil, sunflower or safflower
3/4 cup Sweet milk (see page 28)

Apple Filling	5 medium (3 inches in diameter) sweet baking apples (Grimes, Golden, Spartan, McIntosh) 1 tsp. cinnamon
Custard	1 cup Nonfat Yogurt (see page 29) or commercial nonfat yogurt 1/2 cup Sweet Milk (see page 28) 2 large eggs, beaten 1 tsp. vanilla

1. Preheat oven to 350 degrees (F).
2. Prepare a 9 x 13-inch baking dish with oil or lecithin/oil. Set aside.
3. In a large bowl combine flour, baking powder, baking soda, salt and light oil. Mix thoroughly.
4. Beat in 3/4 cup Sweet Milk (see page 28) to complete biscuit pastry.
5. Pat the biscuit dough into the prepared pan, spreading it evenly across the bottom and about 1/2-inch up the sides of the pan.
6. Bake for 5 minutes at 350 degrees. Set aside to cool.
7. Meanwhile prepare Apple Filling. Wash, core and slice enough apples to equal 5 cups. Leave peels intact if the apples are un-waxed. They provide their own sweetness and flavor.
8. Toss apples with cinnamon in a large bowl.
9. Arrange apples in cooled biscuit crust.
10. Prepare Custard by beating together yogurt, Sweet Milk, eggs and vanilla.
11. Pour custard over apples in crust.
12. Bake kuchen at 350 degrees for 45 minutes.
13. Serve warm or cold.

Variations   Apple-Raisin Kuchen: use 4 cups sliced apples and 1 cup raisins in place of 5 cups apples. Proceed as recipe directs.

Pear Kuchen: use pears in place of apples. Bake as recipe directs.

Nutritional information   (Apple Kuchen and Pear Kuchen) per serving (1/15), 144 calories, 1 fat, 1/2 fruit, 1/2 milk (nonfat), 1/2 bread exchanges
(Apple-Raisin) per serving (1/15), 160 calories, 1 fruit, 1 fat, 1/2 bread, 1/2 milk (nonfat) exchange

Apple Struedel

Preparation time   1 hour to prepare and bake
Yield   9 (2 x 3-inch) servings

Ingredients
Pastry
    2/3 cup whole wheat flour
    1/3 cup Blended Butter (see page 26)
      or 1/6 cup oil and 1/6 cup butter
    1 large egg
    1 T. apple cider vinegar

Filling
    2 cups (10 ounces) sliced, unpeeled apples (Grimes Golden, Jonathon, McIntosh, Cortland, etc.)
    3 T. raisins
    2 T. finely chopped walnuts
    1/8 tsp. cinnamon

1. Early in day or day before baking, in a medium sized bowl, measure 2/3 cup flour. With two table knives or a pastry blade cut in blended butter (butter/oil) until mixture is coarse.
2. Beat in egg and vinegar to make a soft, sticky dough.
3. Scrape dough onto a sheet of waxed paper, pat it into an oval, wrap tightly and chill several hours or overnight.
4. On baking day, prepare filling. In a medium sized bowl, gently toss together fruit, nuts and cinnamon, set aside.
5. Remove pastry from refrigerator. Roll out pastry between two 12 x 20-inch long sheets of waxed paper to a 12 x 9-inch rectangle (see illustration).
6. Carefully peel off the top sheet of waxed paper.
7. Transfer the bottom sheet with the pastry on it to a long baking sheet (illustration 2) pastry side up.
8. Spoon the filling down the pastry to within 2 inches of the side nearest you. (illustration 3)
9. Lift edge of waxed paper nearest you, and with a table knife or rubber scraper, gently separate pastry from paper. (illustration 4)
10. Continue lifting paper and rolling struedel away from you, carefully separating pastry from paper as you go until waxed paper has been completely removed and struedel is resting on baking sheet. Perfect! Right? If not, pinch together any gaps in the pastry. (A gap here and there is ok anyway—they will allow steam to escape during baking.)
11. Gently tuck ends under and pinch to seal (illustration 5).
12. Bake at 375 degrees for 30 minutes or until pastry is lightly browned and filling is tender.
13. Slice into 9 2 x 3-inch pieces and serve warm or cold. (illustration 6)

Variations Peach/Pear Struedel: substitute 2 cups sliced peaches or pears for the 2 cups sliced apples. Proceed as recipe directs.

Cherry Struedel: substitute 2 1/4 cups pitted sweet cherries for apples and raisins. Substitute 2 T. sliced almonds for 2 T. walnuts. Proceed as recipe directs.

Nutritional information (Apple, Peach/Pear, Cherry Struedels) per serving, 141 calories, 1 fruit, 1 fat and 1/4 meat (high fat) exchange

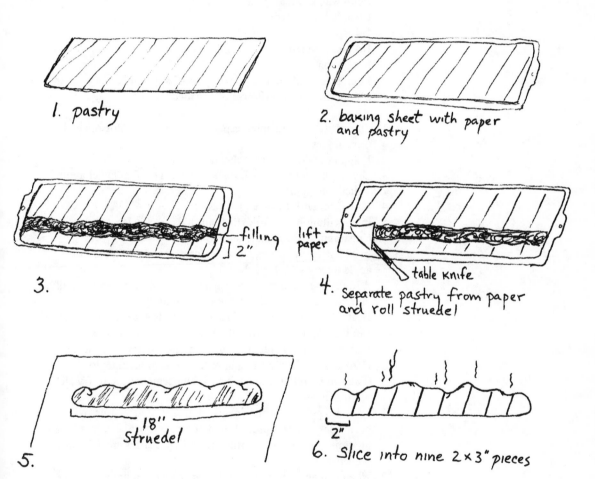

1. pastry

2. baking sheet with paper and pastry

3. — filling] 2"

4. lift paper — table knife. Separate pastry from paper and roll struedel

5. 18" Struedel

6. slice into nine 2×3" pieces 2"

Apple Plumps

Preparation time   30-40 minutes
Yield   serves 5

These soft, warm apple rounds are a treat, especially during football weather. They make a meal in themselves when served with lowfat plain yogurt, cottage cheese or a wedge of sharp cheddar.

Ingredients

3 medium apples (2 1/2 inches in diameter)
1 cup whole wheat flour
1 tsp. baking powder
1/4 tsp. salt
1/4 tsp. cinnamon
1 large egg
1 cup skim milk or 1 cup unsweetened apple juice
2 T. sunflower or safflower oil, divided

1. Thoroughly wash apples, especially at core and blossom ends. Core apples.
2. If apples are waxed, peel them.
3. Slice apples into 1/4-inch thick circles. You should get about 7 slices per apple.
4. Blot slices with towel and set aside.
5. In a medium bowl, fork stir flour, baking powder, salt and cinnamon, to combine. Set aside.
6. In a large bowl beat egg until lemony, then beat in milk or apple juice and 1 T. of the oil.
7. Add dry ingredients to the egg mixture and beat well until all ingredients are mixed and there are no lumps.
8. Heat 1 T. oil in a heavy skillet (cast iron is excellent for this). Pan is ready when a drop of batter in the skillet sizzles.
9. With a fork, dip apple slices into batter, coating both sides.
10. Place coated slice in pan and reduce heat to medium low. (Pan should retain enough heat at this temperature to fry all of your slices.)
11. Fry until golden, turning gently with a slotted spatula to cook both sides. Repeat procedure with the rest of the apples. Frying time depends on the thickness of your slices and how hot your pan is.
12. When golden, remove apples to paper towel to drain.
13. Serve warm.

Variation   **Pineapple Plumps:** Use pineapple slices, packed in their own juice, in place of apple slices. Drain pineapple well, reserving juice, pat each slice dry with towelling. Use 1 cup of the reserved unsweetened pineapple juice in place of the 1 cup apple juice in the batter.

(Apple Plumps) per serving (4 rounds) made with milk, 190 calories or 1 fruit, 1 fat, 1 milk (nonfat) and 1/2 bread exchanges
1 serving (4 rounds) made with apple juice, 200 calories or 2 fruits, 1 fat, 1/2 meat (medium fat) and 1/2 bread exchange

Peach Crisp

Preparation time   45 minutes to prepare and bake
Yield   5 cups or 9 servings

Ingredients

3 cups sliced fresh, frozen or canned (without sugar)
   peaches (2 pounds)
1/2 cup dried currants
1/4 tsp. cinnamon
1/4 tsp. nutmeg
1/3 cup old fashioned oatmeal or triticale, or whole wheat
   flakes—or a combination
2 T. butter, room temperature
2 T. light oil, safflower or sunflower
2 T. water

1. Heat oven to 375 degrees (F).
2. Arrange peach slices in an 8 x 8-inch baking dish.
3. Sprinkle with currants, cinnamon, and nutmeg.
4. In a small bowl combine remaining ingredients, mixture should be crumbly.
5. Sprinkle crumbly mixture over peaches and currants.
6. Bake for 30 minutes or until peaches are tender.
7. Serve warm or cold. Delicious with a wedge of cheese, a dollop of Cinnamon Yogurt (see page 131) or a tall glass of milk.
8. Refrigerate leftovers covered.

Nutritional information   per serving, 126 calories, 1 fruit, 1 fat, 1/2 bread exchanges

Peach Kuchen

Preparation time	1 1/2 hours to prepare and bake
Yield	serves 15 (9 x 13-inch pan)

Ingredients
Biscuit Crust

2 cups whole wheat flour
2 tsp. baking powder
1 tsp. baking soda
1/2 tsp. salt
1/4 cup light oil, sunflower or safflower
3/4 cup Sweet Milk (see page 28)

Peach filling

1 1/2 pounds fresh or frozen (without sugar) peaches
1 cup raisins
1/4 tsp. cinnamon
1/4 tsp. nutmeg

Custard

1 cup Nonfat Yogurt (see page 29)
   or commercial plain yogurt
1/2 cup Sweet Milk
2 large eggs, beaten
1 tsp. vanilla

1. Preheat oven to 350 degrees (F).
2. Prepare a 9 x 13-inch pan with oil or lecithin/oil and set aside.
3. In a large bowl combine flour, baking powder, baking soda, salt and light oil. Mix thoroughly.
4. Beat in 3/4 cup Sweet Milk to complete the biscuit pastry.
5. Pat the biscuit dough into the prepared pan, spreading it evenly across the bottom and about 1/2-inch up the sides of the pan.
6. Bake for 5 minutes at 350 degrees. Set aside to cool.
7. Meanwhile prepare Peach Filling by peeling, pitting and slicing peaches to equal 4 cups.
8. In a large bowl gently toss together peach slices, raisins, cinnamon and nutmeg.
9. Arrange Peach Filling in cooled biscuit crust.
10. Prepare custard by beating together yogurt, 1/2 cup Sweet Milk, eggs and vanilla.
11. Pour custard over filled crust.
12. Bake at 350 degrees for 45 minutes.
13. Serve warm or cold.

Variations

Melba Kuchen: substitute 1 cup raspberries for raisins in Peach Kuchen. Bake as directed.
Blueberry-Peach Kuchen: substitute 1 cup blueberries for raisins in Peach Kuchen. Bake as directed.

Nutritional information   (Peach Kuchen) per serving (1/15), 158 calories, 1 fat, 1 fruit, 1/2 milk (nonfat), 1/2 bread exchange.
(Melba Kuchen) per serving, 140 calories, 1 fat, 1/2 fruit, 1/2 milk (nonfat), 1/2 bread exchanges.
(Blueberry-Peach Kuchen) per serving, 140 calories, 1 fat, 1/2 fruit, 1/2 milk (nonfat), 1/2 bread exchanges

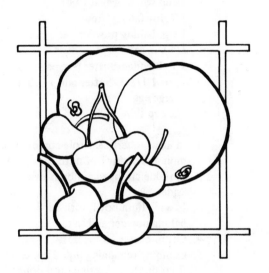

Peach Spoon Out

Preparation time 20 minutes to prepare, 40 minutes to bake
Yield 2 quarts, serves 12

Ingredients

7 cups sliced, fresh or frozen (without sugar) peaches
1/2 cup chopped almonds
1 tsp. cinnamon, divided
pinch nutmeg
1 cup whole wheat flour
1 T. lowfat soy flour
1 tsp. baking powder
1/4 tsp. salt
3 T. Blended Butter (see page 26)
   or 1 1/2 T. butter and 1 1/2 T. oil
1 large egg
1/2 cup skim milk

1. In a two quart casserole combine peaches with 1/2 tsp. cinnamon and a pinch of nutmeg, stirring gently.
2. Sprinkle chopped almonds over the fruit and set the casserole aside.
3. In a medium bowl, fork stir flours, 1/2 tsp. cinnamon, 1 tsp. baking powder and salt.
4. Cut in butter.
5. Combine remaining liquid ingredients and add them to the flour mixture, stirring until dough is uniform.
6. Patiently spread the dough out over the peaches. Some peaches will peek through the batter.
7. Cover the casserole and bake at 400 degrees for 30 minutes.
8. Uncover and continue baking 10-15 minutes until browned and inserted cake tester comes out clean.
9. Spoon out warm, into serving dishes and top with a dollop of yogurt if desired.
10. Refrigerate leftovers, covered.

Nutritional information per serving, 143 calories, 1 fruit, 1/2 meat (high fat), 1/2 bread, 1/3 fat exchanges

CHAPTER EIGHT
Pies

Basic Pie Crust

**1 Crust Pie
Ingredients**

1/2 cup whole wheat flour
1/2 cup unbleached flour
1/4 tsp. salt
1/3 cup light oil (sunflower or safflower)
2 T. ice water

1. In a medium bowl, fork stir flours and salt to mix.
2. Combine oil and ice water in a measuring cup. Then pour it into the flour mixture.
3. Stir all ingredients just until dough leaves the sides of the bowl. Form it into a large ball.
4. On a pastry board or waxed paper covered surface, flatten dough, patting it into a large circle.
5. Cover the pastry with another sheet of waxed paper and with a rolling pin, roll it out to the desired size.
6. Gently peel off top sheet of paper.
7. With pie plate next to pastry, lift furthest edge of paper and pastry across pie plate (I work from right to left), inverting paper so that pastry is closest to pie plate and paper topside.
8. Settle pastry into plate, carefully peeling paper from pastry. Tear paper off in strips if necessary.
9. Arrange pastry in plate, fluting edges with fingers or a fork.
10. If baking empty shell, prick with fork to prevent bubbles.
11. Bake at 400 degrees for 15 minutes. Cool before filling.

**2 Crust Pie
Ingredients**

1 cup whole wheat flour
1 cup unbleached flour
1/2 tsp. salt
1/2 cup light oil (sunflower or safflower)
1/4 cup ice water

1. Proceed as for 1 crust pie, dividing dough in half and repeating the same procedure for bottom and top crusts.

Nutritional information

per 1 crust shell, 1059 calories or 12 fat, 8 bread exchanges.
per 1/9th pie crust, 118 calories, 1 fat exchange, 1 bread exchange.
per 2 crust shell, 1796 calories or 16 fat, 16 bread exchanges.
per 1/12th of 2 crust pie, 149 calories or 1 fat, 1 1/2 bread exchanges.

Coconut Pie Shell

Coconut is the fruit of a palm, although nutritionally it is considered a nut. This naturally sweet substance can be found packaged, with no sugar added, in most grocery stores. This recipe requires a finely flaked coconut. If only large (1/4 x 1/2-inch) coconut flakes are available in your area, they can be chopped, rolled under a rolling pin or grated to a fine powder in your blender.

This recipe is not recommended for a two crust pie as the amount of natural oil in the coconut predisposes it to browning more quickly than the other ingredients in the pastry. The result is a burned top crust or an underbaked bottom crust.

1 Crust Pie Ingredients

1/2 cup whole wheat flour
3/8 cup unbleached flour
2 T. unsweetened coconut flakes
1/4 tsp. salt
1/3 cup light oil (sunflower or safflower)
2 T. ice water

1. In a medium sized bowl, fork stir flours, coconut and salt until thoroughly mixed. Set aside.
2. In a measuring cup, combine oil and water and pour it over the dry ingredients, stirring with a fork.
3. When pastry pulls away from bowl, shape it into a ball and flatten it on a pastry board or wax paper covered surface.
4. Pat pastry into a large circle, cover with another sheet of wax paper and roll out to desired size.
5. Gently peel off top sheet of paper.
6. With pie plate next to pastry, lift furthest edge of paper and pastry across pie plate, inverting paper so that pastry is closest to pie plate and paper is topside.
7. Carefully peel paper from pastry, tearing paper off in strips if necessary.
8. Arrange pastry in plate, fluting edges with fingers or a fork.
9. If baking this shell empty, prick it in several places with the tines of a fork to prevent puckering.
10. Bake at 375 degrees for about 15 minutes.
11. Cool before filling.

Nutritional information per 10-inch pie shell, 1080 calories, 7 1/2 bread, 10 fat exchanges.
per 1/10, 1 serving coconut shell, 108 calories, 3/4 bread, 1 fat exchange.

Wheat Germ Crust

This pastry has a nutty flavor that complements cream and fruit pies. It is more difficult to handle but can be patted into the pie plate instead of being rolled out.

1 Crust Pie Ingredients

1/4 cup wheat germ
1/4 cup whole wheat flour
1/2 cup unbleached flour
1/4 tsp. salt
1/3 cup light oil (safflower or sunflower oil)
2 T. ice water

1. In a medium sized bowl, fork stir wheat germ, flours and salt until thoroughly mixed.
2. Combine oil and water in a measuring cup then pour it into the dry ingredients, stirring with a fork, until all ingredients are moistened.
3. Roll it out, following directions (4-11) for Basic Pie Shell, or pat it into the pie plate following directions (4-5) for Whole Wheat Crust.

Nutritional information

per crust, 956 calories or 8 fat, 8 bread exchanges.
per 1/8 of crust, 119 calories or 1 fat, 1 bread exchange.

Whole Wheat Crust

This simple and wholesome crust is patted into the pie plate. For a streusel-like topping, a second crust can be crumbled over the top of the filling before baking.

1 Crust Pie Ingredients

1 cup whole wheat flour
1/4 tsp. salt
1/4 cup light oil (sunflower or safflower)
2 T. ice water

1. In a medium bowl, fork stir flour and salt to thoroughly mix.
2. Combine oil and water in a measuring cup and pour it into the flour mixture.
3. Stir until all ingredients are moistened.
4. Pour the pastry mixture into a pie plate and flatten it across the bottom and up the sides of the plate using your fingers, the back of a spoon or the back of an empty measuring cup. Be careful to distribute the pastry evenly.
5. To bake empty shell, bake at 400 degrees for 15 minutes.

Nutritional information

per 1 crust, 906 calories or 6 bread, 12 fat exchanges.
per 1/12 of crust, 76 calories or 1/2 bread, 1 fat exchange.

Apple Pie Filling

Preparation time   1 1/2 hours to prepare and bake
Yield   serves 12

Ingredients   pastry for a 2 crust pie—Basic Pie Crust (see page 105)

5-6 small baking apples (2 1/2 inches in diameter)
1/2 cup coarsely chopped raisins
1/2 cup coarsely chopped walnuts
cinnamon
nutmeg

1. Preheat oven to 375 degrees (F) and prebake shell for 5 minutes. Cool to room temperature. (Set aside 1/2 the dough for the top of the pie.)
2. Thoroughly wash 5-6 medium apples, peeling only if they have been waxed.
3. Core apples and slice about 1/4-inch thin.
4. In a large bowl combine raisins, nuts, apples, cinnamon, and nutmeg, tossing gently to mix.
5. Pour apple mixture into prepared pastry.
6. Carefully cover with second half of pastry, rolled out. Slit top crust in a few places with a sharp knife to allow steam to escape.
7. Bake at 375 degrees for 45 minutes or until apples are tender.
8. Serve warm or cold.
9. Refrigerate any leftover portions.

Variations   *Berry Pie Filling:* use 3 cups fresh or frozen berries and 1/2 tsp. almond extract in place of the apples, nuts and raisins.
Peach Pie Filling: use 5-6 medium size, very ripe peaches or 20 ounces unsweetened frozen peaches and 1/2 tsp. of cinnamon. Cut peaches into chunks.
Pear Pie Filling: use 5 medium (3 1/2 x 2 1/2-inches in diameter), very ripe pears, 1/2 cup chopped raisins and a pinch of nutmeg. Cut pears into chunks.

Nutritional information   (Apple) per serving (1/12 pie), 225 calories or 1 1/2 bread, 2 fat, 1 fruit exchanges
(Berry, Peach) per serving (1/12 pie), 165 calories or 1 1/2 bread, 1 fat, 1/2 fruit exchanges
(Pear) per serving (1/12 pie), 208 calories or 1 1/2 bread, 1 1/2 fat and 1 fruit exchanges

Pumpkin Pie Filling

I bake my own pumpkin. It seems to be naturally sweeter than canned pumpkin. Here's how I do it:

a) Scrub a small firm pumpkin, removing the stem.

b) Split pumpkin in half and scrape sides to remove seeds and membrane.

c) Place pumpkin halves face down on an oil or lecithin/oil prepared baking sheet and bake at 375 degrees for 30 minutes or until tender.

d) Cool pumpkin until manageable, then scrape soft pulp away from pumpkin peel.

e) Spoon pulp into measuring cup and suitable freezer container.

f) Freeze the extra pumpkin for later use.

Preparation time 1 1/2 hours to prepare and bake

Yield 1 9-inch pie, 12 pie servings, 8 custard servings

Ingredients
1 10-inch unbaked Basic Pie Crust (see page 105)
1 can pumpkin pulp (2 cups)
3 large eggs
1/4 cup packed, pitted dates (10)
1 cup Sweet Milk (see page 28)
1 cup Applesauce (see page 25)
    or commercial unsweetened applesauce
1 tsp. vanilla
1 tsp. cinnamon
3/4 tsp. salt
1/8 tsp. cloves
1/8 tsp. ginger
1/8 tsp. nutmeg

1. Combine pumpkin, eggs and dates in blender. Puree until dates are ground fine.

2. Add sweet milk and applesauce and blend again until mixture is smooth and uniform.

3. Add vanilla and seasonings, mixing well. Set aside.

4. Pour pumpkin filling into unbaked pie shell and bake at 425 degrees for 15 minutes. Lower heat and finish baking at 350 degrees for 40-45 minutes. Cover with foil the last 20 minutes or so to keep a nice pumpkin color.

5. For pumpkin custard, prepare pumpkin filling as for pie. Pour the filling into a two quart casserole or eight individual custard cups. Bake at 425 degrees for 15 minutes and 350 degrees for 30-40 minutes. The cupped custard will take a shorter time to bake.

6. Refrigerate pie/custard until thoroughly chilled. Serve cold.

Nutritional information per 1/12 of pie, 153 calories or 1 fat, 1 fruit, 1 bread exchange.
per custard cup, 98 calories or 1 bread (starchy vegetable), 1/2 fat exchange.

Banana Cream Pie

Preparation time   1 1/2 hours to prepare, 1 hour to chill
Yield   1 deep dish 10-inch pie, 10 servings

Ingredients
1 T. unflavored gelatin or 4 T. agar flakes
1 T. lemon juice
1/2 cup boiling water
1 cup nonfat milk (skim)
1 10-inch Coconut Pie Shell (see page 106)
1 cup Nonfat Yogurt (see page 29)
   or 1 cup commercial nonfat yogurt
1/2 tsp. vanilla
6 small (7 3/4-inch) bananas, very ripe
nutmeg

1. Put gelatin or agar flakes into a small bowl and add lemon juice to soften.
2. Boil water and stir it into the gelatin until the gelatin is completely dissolved.
3. Add 1 cup nonfat milk to the dissolved gelatin, stirring until well combined.
4. Refrigerate milk/gelatin for 45-60 minutes or until thickened. Meanwhile, prepare crust.
5. Bake Coconut Crust. Set it aside to cool to room temperature.
6. After the milk has gelled, scrape it into the blender, add Nonfat Yogurt and vanilla. Peel three of the small, very ripe bananas and add them to the blender.
7. Process until mixture is smooth. Set aside.
8. Peel and slice the remaining three bananas and layer them evenly in the prepared crust.
9. Pour the blender mixture over the layered bananas and sprinkle with nutmeg.
10. Refrigerate 1 hour or until thoroughly chilled.
11. Serve cold.

For Pudding   Halve the filling ingredients to make five 1/2-cup servings. Fold sliced bananas into the blended yogurt mixture and spoon pudding into individual serving dishes or a 2 1/2 cup bowl. Chill until serving time.

Nutritional information   (Banana Cream Pie) per serving (1/10), 172 calories or 1 fruit, 1 fat, 3/4 bread, 1/4 milk (nonfat) exchange
(Pudding) per serving (1/2 cup), 67 calories or 1/3 milk (nonfat) and 1 fruit exchanges

Glazed Berry Pie

Preparation time   1 hour to prepare, 2 hours to chill
Yield   1 9-inch pie, 12 servings

Ingredients   **pastry for 2 crust pie, Basic Pie Crust (see page 105)**

3 cups fresh or frozen (without sugar) strawberries, blueberries, raspberries, sweet cherries or any combination
1/2 tsp. almond extract for cherries, strawberries and raspberries
   or pinch of cinnamon and cloves to blueberries
1 1/2 tsp. unflavored gelatin

1. Arrange bottom crust in pie shell, prick with fork tines and set aside.
2. Preheat oven to 475 degrees (F).
3. Roll out top crust.
4. Using a cookie cutter, cut out shapes from rolled top crust (I like to make star shapes), place crust shapes on cookie sheet and bake along with pie shell, at 475 degrees for 8-10 minutes.
5. Remove from oven to rack, gently, and cool.

Berry Filling

6. Put berries into a saucepan. Cover and cook on low heat about 10 minutes. Do not add water.
7. Remove lid and bring to a boil. Remove from heat.
8. Remove lid and bri
8. Spoon some of the hot juice into a small bowl. Stir in gelatin, until it dissolves.
9. Return the gelatin-juice to the hot berries. Stir gently to mix gelatin throughout berries.
10. Allow filling to cool to lukewarm before pouring it into the pie shell.
11. Arrange crust shapes on top and refrigerate at least 2 hours before serving.

Variation   use 2 cups fresh or frozen strawberries and 1 cup drained canned pineapple in place of the 3 cups of strawberries.

Nutritional information   per serving (1/12 of pie), 163 calories, 1/2 fruit, 1 fat, 1 1/2 bread exchanges.
(Strawberry Pineapple) per serving (1/12 pie), 170 calories or 2/3 fruit, 1 fat, 1 1/2 bread exchanges

Cherry Custard Pie

Preparation time   20 minutes to prepare, 50-60 minutes to bake
Yield   1 9-inch pie, serves 10

Ingredients   1 Wheat Germ Crust (see page 107)

1 1/2 cups Sweet Milk (see page 28)
3 large eggs
1/2 tsp. vanilla
1/8 tsp. nutmeg
1/8 tsp. salt
3 cups fresh or frozen (without sugar) pitted, sour cherries
1 T. unflavored gelatin

1. Combine, until thoroughly blended, Sweet Milk, eggs, vanilla, nutmeg and salt.
2. Pour the custard into the unbaked pie shell and bake at 300 degrees on the oven shelf that is just below the oven center, for 50-60 minutes or until knife inserted in center comes out clean. While pie is baking, prepare Cherry Topping.
3. In a covered saucepan over low heat, warm cherries for ten minutes.
4. Remove lid and raise heat, bringing cherries to a boil.
5. Measure 1 T. unflavored gelatin into a small bowl. Spoon about 2 T. of the boiling juice into the gelatin to soften it.
6. Stir to prevent lumps, adding more cherry juice until gelatin is completely dissolved.
7. Pour the dissolved gelatin into the pan of hot cherries. Boil, stirring for two minutes. (This is a good time to look for stray cherry pits—I usually find 3 or 4.)
8. Remove fruit from heat and let cool to room temperature.
9. When pie has finished baking, remove it to a rack and allow it to cool to room temperature.
10. Spoon cooled fruit on top of the cooled custard pie—spreading it evenly and to the edges.
11. Refrigerate 90 minutes or until thoroughly chilled.
12. Cut into ten pieces and serve.

Variations   Replace cherries with strawberries, peaches or other fresh or frozen fruit.

Nutritional information   per serving (1/10), 162 calories, 1 fruit, 3/4 bread, 2/3 meat (high fat) exchanges

Cranberry-Raisin Pie

Preparation time a little over 1 hour to prepare and bake

Yield 1 9-inch pie or 10 servings

Ingredients

4 cups whole raw cranberries (or 1 16-ounce package frozen without sugar)
4 small (2 1/2-inches in diameter) sweet baking apples
1 cup raisins
1 tsp. cinnamon
1/2 cup water
1 1/2 T. tapioca
Basic Pie Crust (see page 105) for 2 crust pie

1. Wash and drain cranberries. Put them in a large saucepan. Set aside.
2. Wash and core apples, leaving peels intact unless waxed. Cut apples into 1-inch chunks.
3. Add apple chunks, raisins, cinnamon and water to cranberries.
4. Cover and cook over low heat for 15 minutes.
5. Uncover and continue to cook on low, stir frequently.
6. Raise heat to medium, stir constantly.
7. When cranberries split, add tapioca, stirring it in.
8. Cook and stir for one full minute.
9. Pour hot filling into unbaked pie shell.
10. Preheat oven to 425 degrees (F).
11. Carefully place top crust over filling. Seal and flute edges. Slit top to allow steam to escape during baking.
12. Bake at 425 degrees for 30 minutes.
13. Serve warm or cold.

Nutritional information per serving (1/10), 268 calories, 2 fruit, 1 1/2 bread, 1 1/2 fat exchanges.

Orange Chiffon Pie

Preparation time	2 hours to prepare, 2 hours to chill
Yield	1 10-inch pie or 10 servings

Ingredients

1 T. unflavored gelatin
2 cups unsweetened orange juice
1 Coconut Pie Shell (see page 106)
1 cup Nonfat Yogurt (see page 29)
   or commercial plain yogurt
1 large orange, peeled
1 cup drained, unsweetened, crushed pineapple
1 T. toasted unsweetened coconut

1. Place in a small bowl 1 T. gelatin.
2. In a saucepan heat orange juice until very hot.
3. Stir enough hot juice into the gelatin to dissolve it. Then stir the dissolved gelatin into the remaining hot juice.
4. Refrigerate gelatin 1 1/2 hours. Meanwhile prepare pie crust.
5. Bake the crust according to directions. Cool to room temperature.
6. When gelatin is thickened, whip in Nonfat Plain Yogurt.
7. Cut orange into 1-inch bite-sized pieces. Stir these pieces and the drained crushed pineapple into the yogurt mixture.
8. Pour filling into the cooled coconut crust. Top with toasted coconut.
9. Refrigerate 2 hours or until set.

Nutritional information   per serving (1/10), 63 calories, 1 fruit, 1/4 nonfat milk exchange.

Tangy Peach Pie

Preparation time 2 hours to prepare, 2 hours to chill
Yield 1 9-inch pie or 9 servings

Ingredients
1 1/4 pound (20 ounces) raw peaches, fresh or frozen
  without sugar
3/4 cup unsweetened apple juice
1 T. unflavored gelatin
9-inch Basic Pie Crust (see page 105)
1/2 cup Nonfat Yogurt (see page 29)
  or commercial plain yogurt
1/2 tsp. cinnamon
1/4 tsp. nutmeg

1. Peel raw peaches. To make them easier to peel, place a rack or steamer in 2 inches of boiling water. Set the peaches on the rack and cover, steaming for 2 or 3 minutes, or until peaches look ready to split skin. Cool. Peels should slide off easily. Discard peels.
2. Slice peaches. Measure out 1 cup of sliced peaches and set the others aside.
3. Combine the 1 cup sliced peaches with 3/4 cup apple juice in the blender.
4. Pour the blended peaches into a medium saucepan and cook over low heat.
5. Place 1 T. gelatin in a small bowl. When peach mixture is very hot, stir some of it into the gelatin and dissolve the gelatin.
6. Empty the dissolved gelatin into the hot peach mixture, stirring well.
7. Refrigerate the peach mixture 1 1/2 hours.
8. Meanwhile bake a pie shell following directions. Allow crust to cool to room temperature.
9. Arrange remaining sliced peaches in pie crust.
10. When peach mixture has been chilled 1 1/2 hours, remove it from the refrigerator and pour it into a mixing bowl.
11. Add nonfat yogurt and cinnamon to gelled peach mixture and whip on high speed until thoroughly blended.
12. Pour whipped mixture over peaches.
13. Garnish and sprinkle nutmeg over all and refrigerate.
14. Chill two hours or until set.

For Pudding Gently fold peaches into whipped yogurt mixture. Spoon into nine 1/2-cup serving dishes or into a large serving bowl. Sprinkle with nutmeg. Chill two hours and serve cold.

Nutritional information (Peach Pie) per serving (1/9 pie), 168 calories, 1 fruit, 1 bread, 1 fat, 1/8 milk (nonfat) exchanges
(Pudding) per serving (1/2 cup), 50 calories or 1 fruit, 1/8 milk (nonfat) exchange

Hippopotamus Pie

Preparation time 2 1/2 hours to prepare, 2 hours to chill
Yield 1 10-inch pie, serves 10

Ingredients

1 Coconut Pie Shell (see page 106)
1 20-ounce can crushed pineapple (packed in its own juice)
2 T. unsweetened coconut flakes
2 T. unflavored gelatin
2 T. cold water
2 large egg whites
1 cup Nonfat Yogurt (see page 29)
   or commercial nonfat yogurt
1/4 tsp. almond extract

1. Bake and cool pie shell according to directions.
2. In a small saucepan combine crushed pineapple and its juice with the coconut. Bring to a boil.
3. Meanwhile, in a small bowl, soften the unflavored gelatin in the 2 T. cold water.
4. When pineapple juice begins to boil, add some of it to the softened gelatin, dissolving the gelatin.
5. Stir the dissolved gelatin into the hot pineapple mixture and remove it from the heat.
6. Chill pineapple mixture 90 minutes.
7. When mixture is thoroughly chilled, whip the egg whites until stiff.
8. Fold the Nonfat Yogurt, almond extract and chilled pineapple into the egg whites; then whip on high speed.
9. Pour the filling into the cooled, baked coconut crust.
10. Refrigerate at least 2 hours before serving.
11. If desired, garnish with a teaspoon of lightly toasted coconut.

Pudding suggestion Pour whipped filling into 6 custard cups or dessert dishes. Chill before serving.

Nutritional information (Pie) per serving (1/10), 162 calories, 1 fruit, 3/4 bread, 1/2 fat, 1/4 milk (whole fat) exchanges
(Pudding) per serving (1/6), 89 calories, 1 fruit, 1/2 milk (nonfat) exchanges

CHAPTER NINE
Puddings

Custard

Preparation time 15 minutes to prepare, 1 hour to bake
Yield 4 servings or fills 1 9-inch pie shell

Ingredients
    1 1/2 cups Sweet Milk (see page 28)
    3 large eggs
    1/2 tsp. vanilla
    1/8 tsp. nutmeg
    1/8 tsp. salt
    nutmeg, garnish

1. Beat or blend all ingredients until thoroughly combined.
2. Pour into 4 custard cups and sprinkle with additional nutmeg.
3. Set the custard cups in a pan of hot water. The water should come within 1 inch of the tops of the cups.
4. Bake on the oven shelf that is just below the oven center.
5. Bake at 300 degrees for 1 hour or until knife inserted in center comes out clean.
6. Cool 20 minutes. Serve warm or cool to room temperature before serving. Or chill in refrigerator and serve cold.

Nutritional information per serving, 105 calories, 1 meat exchange (medium fat), 2/3 fruit exchange.

Raisin Bread Pudding

Preparation time   1 hour to prepare and bake
Yield   serves 8 (1/2 cup servings)

Ingredients   3 small (2 1/2-inch in diameter) apples—Cortland, Spartan, Grimes Golden or other sweet baking apples
3 slices Raisin Bread (see page 33) or commercial raisin bread
2 large eggs
1 cup Applesauce (see page 25)
   or commercial natural style applesauce
1 cup Sweet Milk (see page 28)
1 tsp. vanilla
1/2 tsp. cinnamon

1. Heat oven to 350 degrees (F).
2. Wash, core and chop apples into 1-inch pieces to equal 2 cups packed.
3. In a 2 quart casserole, layer chopped apples, then slices of raisin bread.
4. In a medium bowl, beat eggs.
5. Add applesauce, Sweet Milk, vanilla and cinnamon, stirring to blend well.
6. Pour egg mixture over bread and apples.
7. Bake at 350 degrees for 40-45 minutes or until apples are tender and pudding is golden.
8. Serve warm or cold. Refrigerate any extra pudding, covered.

Nutritional information   per serving (1/2 cup), 90 calories or 1 bread and 1/3 fat exchanges.

Old Fashioned Bread Pudding

This moist, steamed bread is traditionally served during the coldest months of the winter. It's a heart warmer.

Preparation time 20 minutes to prepare, 2 1/2 hours to steam
Yield 24 servings

Ingredients
1 cup Sweet Milk (see page 28)
1 cup packed, chopped dates
2 cups whole wheat flour
1/2 tsp. baking soda
1/4 tsp. salt
1 cup raisins

1. Fill a large kettle with about 3 inches of water, place rack in kettle and heat water to boiling as you prepare batter.
2. Oil a 1 1/2 quart earthenware bowl or souffle dish that will fit inside of kettle. Set prepared bowl aside.
3. Puree Sweet Milk and dates in blender. Set aside.
4. In large bowl combine flour, soda and salt.
5. Mix puree into dry ingredients.
6. Stir in raisins.
7. Put in earthenware bowl and cover with foil, shiny side down.
8. Place foil covered bowl on steamer in kettle of boiling water. Reduce heat to low and cover kettle.
9. Steam over low heat for about 2 1/2 hours.
10. Chill, slice into 24 pieces and serve. This freezes well.

Note To keep track of the 2 1/2 hours steaming time, it helps me to write down the starting time and finished steaming time. Once I get working on something else, it's so easy to forget when I put the bread in and when it should be finished.

Nutritional information 1/24 of recipe (1 slice), 75 calories or 1 bread exchange.

Plum Pudding

Preparation time 25 minutes to prepare, 2 1/2 hours to steam
Yield serves 24

Ingredients

1 1/2 cups whole wheat flour
1 1/2 tsp. baking soda
1/2 tsp. salt
1 tsp. cinnamon
1/2 tsp. nutmeg
1/2 tsp. cloves
1 cup skim milk
1/2 tsp. vanilla extract
2/3 cup packed, pitted dates
1/3 cup Blended Butter (see page 26)
    or 1/6 cup oil and 1/6 cup butter
3 large eggs
1 1/2 cups whole wheat bread crumbs
1 cup pitted and chopped prunes
2 cups raisins
1 cup chopped walnuts

1. Set a rack or invert a steamer and place it in a large kettle
   Fill the kettle with about 4 inches water and heat it
   to boiling.
2. Oil an earthenware 2 quart bowl or souffle dish and set it aside
   with a piece of aluminum foil that will cover it securely.
3. In a large bowl combine flour, baking soda, salt and spices.
   Set aside.
4. In the blender, on high, process milk, vanilla, dates, Blended
   Butter (or oil and butter to equal 1/3 cup), and eggs until
   dates are finely chopped.
5. Pour blended mixture into dry ingredients. Then stir in bread
   crumbs, prunes, raisins and nuts until evenly moistened.
6. Turn batter into the prepared bowl or dish and cover with foil
   (dull side up—shiny side closest to batter).
7. Set on the rack in the furiously boiling water. Cover the entire
   thing with the kettle lid and reduce the heat to low.
8. Steam the pudding for 2 1/2 hours or until center of pudding
   springs back when lightly touched.
9. Slice and serve hot or cold.

Nutritional information per serving (1/24), 180 calories, 1 fruit, 1 bread, 1/2 meat (high fat), 1/2 fat exchanges

Raisin Kugel

Preparation time	1 hour
Yield	12 1/2-cup servings

Ingredients

1/2 pound medium egg noodles (about 4 cups cooked)
1 cup lowfat (2% fat) cottage cheese
2 large eggs
1/2 cup Nonfat Yogurt (see page 29)
   or commercial plain yogurt
2 T. light oil, sunflower or safflower
1 cup raisins, divided
1/4 tsp. salt
1 tsp. vanilla
1 tsp. cinnamon
pinch nutmeg

1. Cook noodles. Over high heat bring 1 1/2 quarts water to a rapid boil. Add noodles and stir. When water returns to boiling, stir again and turn down heat to medium. Cook noodles four or five minutes, stirring often to prevent sticking. Drain noodles in colander and run cold water over them to keep them separate. Set aside to drain while you prepare the rest of the dessert.
2. Heat oven to 350 degrees (F).
3. Prepare a 2 quart casserole with oil or lecithin/oil.
4. In blender, process cottage cheese, eggs, yogurt, oil, 1/4 cup of the raisins, salt, vanilla and cinnamon until mixture is smooth and uniform.
5. In a large bowl, gently fold together drained noodles, the blended cottage cheese mixture and 3/4 cup raisins.
6. Pour mixture into prepared casserole, sprinkle with nutmeg.
7. Bake at 350 degrees for 40 minutes.
8. Serve warm or cold. Refrigerate extras, covered.

Nutritional information   per 1/2 cup serving, 163 calories, 1 meat (medium fat), 1 bread and 1/2 fruit exchange

Matzo Kugel

A rich pudding for Passover.

Preparation time   90 minutes to prepare and bake
Yield   12 servings

Ingredients

3 whole wheat matzos
water
1/2 tsp. salt
1 1/2 T. butter, melted
1/2 cup Apple Butter (see page 24)
   or commercial unsweetened apple butter
3 large eggs, separated
grated rind and juice of 1 lemon
1 1/2 cups Applesauce (see page 25)
   or commercial natural style applesauce
1/2 cup chopped walnuts
1/4 tsp. cinnamon

1. Crumble matzos into a large bowl and add enough water to cover them. Soak until softened, about 10-15 minutes.
2. Drain off extra water.
3. With mixer or large spoon, beat until creamy.
4. Stir in salt and melted butter.
5. Beat in apple butter, egg yolks, lemon rind and juice. Set aside.
6. Beat egg whites until stiff.
7. Fold egg whites into matzo mixture.
8. In a 1 1/2 quart baking dish layer half of matzo batter, chunky applesauce and walnuts. Top with remaining half of batter.
9. Sprinkle with cinnamon.
10. Bake uncovered at 350 degrees for 30 minutes or until lightly browned.
11. Serve warm or cold. Refrigerate unused portions, covered.

Nutritional information   per 1/2 cup serving, 113 calories, 1 fruit, 1/2 meat (high fat), 1/3 fat exchanges.

Apple Tapioca

Preparation time   30 minutes to prepare, 2 hours to chill
Yield   2 cups or 6 1/3-cup servings

Ingredients

2 1/2 cups unsweetened apple juice
1/4 tsp. cinnamon
1/4 cup tapioca (quick cooking)

1. In a large saucepan, combine apple juice and cinnamon.
2. Stir in tapioca and let it soak for five minutes.
3. Over medium heat, bring tapioca to a boil, stirring frequently to prevent sticking.
4. Boil and stir for a full 2 minutes.
5. Cool 20 minutes, then stir again.
6. Transfer tapioca to a serving bowl or individual dishes.
7. Chill two or more hours before serving.
8. Just before serving, garnish with a thin, curled apple wedge, if desired.

Variation   Use orange juice instead of apple juice. Omit cinnamon. After cooking the tapioca, fold in one 11-ounce can of mandarin oranges, drained, or one cup orange sections. Garnish with sprigs of fresh mint. Makes nine 1/3 cup servings.

Nutritional information   per 1/3 cup serving, 69 calories, 1 3/4 fruit exchange.
(Mandarin Tapioca) per 1/3 cup serving, 57 calories, 1 1/2 fruit exchanges

Carob Pudding

Preparation time   1 hour to prepare, 1 hour to chill
Yield   3 1/2 cups or 7 1/2-cup servings

Ingredients

    1 cup packed, pitted dates (about 40)
    2 large eggs, separated
    1 cup skim milk
    3 T. carob powder
    1/4 tsp. cinnamon
    1 cup Nonfat Yogurt (see page 29)
      or commercial plain yogurt
    1 tsp. vanilla extract

1. In blender, process dates, egg yolks and milk—a noisy procedure—until dates are finely chopped.
2. Add carob powder and cinnamon, blend again.
3. Pour blended carob mixture into a saucepan. Place over low heat. Cook, stirring constantly for 15 minutes.
4. Put hot carob mixture in the refrigerator to cool, about 15 minutes, or until you can comfortably rest your hand against the bottom of the pan. When cool, proceed.
5. In a large mixing bowl beat egg whites until stiff.
6. Whip yogurt and vanilla into egg whites.
7. Then fold in cooled carob mixture until thoroughly combined.
8. Pour into 7 individual serving dishes or a large serving bowl. Chill at least 1 hour before serving.

Variations   *Carob Pie:* make and bake an 8-inch pie shell. Cool. Fill with Carob Pudding. Chill to set several hours or overnight.
Carob Ice Milk: freeze the pudding in ice cube trays for 1 1/2 hours or until frozen hard. Place pudding in large bowl and beat well. Return ice cube trays to freezer and refreeze. Serve cold.

Nutritional information   per 1/2 cup serving, 116 calories or 1 fruit, 1 fat, 1/2 milk (whole milk), 1/2 bread exchanges.

Rice Pudding

Preparation time 1 hour
Yield 1 1/3 cups or 4 servings

Ingredients
    2 cups water
    2/3 cup raw brown rice
    1 cup Sweet Milk (see page 28)
    1/4 cup raisins

1. Rinse rice in cold water, draining off any bits that rise to the top. Rinse again, draining well. Set aside.
2. In a heavy bottomed saucepan heat water to boiling.
3. Add rice, stir and cover. Turn heat down to low and steam rice for 45 minutes.
4. Remove lid and stir sweet milk into cooked rice. Raise heat to high and cook, stirring constantly for a full three minutes or until most of the milk is absorbed.
5. Stir in the raisins and spoon pudding into serving dishes.
6. Serve warm or cold.

Variations *Banana Pudding:* After you have added the Sweet Milk and it has been absorbed, add 3/4 cup mashed ripe banana and 1/8 tsp. nutmeg. Combine. Do not use raisins.
Blueberries and Rice Pudding: Use 1 cup plain Nonfat Yogurt in place of Sweet Milk. Add it to 1 cup cooled cooked brown rice. Stir in 1 cup fresh blueberries, 10 chopped almonds and 1/2 teaspoon almond extract. Omit the raisins.

Nutritional information (Rice Pudding) per 1/3 cup serving, 135 calories or 1 bread, 1 fruit, and 1/4 milk (nonfat) exchanges
(Banana Pudding) per 1/3 cup serving, 123 calories or 1 bread, 1 fruit, and 1/8 milk (nonfat) exchanges
(Blueberries and Rice) per 3/4 cup serving, 94 calories or 1/2 milk (nonfat), 1/2 bread, and 1/2 fruit exchanges

Sandcastle Pudding

Preparation time 45 minutes to prepare, 1 hour to chill
Yield 4 cups or 8 1/2-cup servings

Ingredients

2 large eggs, separated
1 cup water
2 cups fresh or frozen sweet corn kernels
1 cup packed, pitted dates
1/4 tsp. salt

1. Beat egg yolks, add water, stir to combine.
2. Put corn and dates in saucepan. Pour water-yolk mixture over all. Stir.
3. Place saucepan over low heat and cook, covered, for 15 minutes.
4. Remove from heat and pour cooked corn date mixture into a blender.
5. Add salt and blend on high until mixture is smooth and uniform.
6. Return blended mixture to the saucepan and cook, uncovered, on low, stirring constantly for 10-12 minutes.
7. Cool pudding mixture in the refrigerator for about 10 minutes or until you can comfortably rest your hand against the bottom of the pan.
8. In large mixing bowl, whip remaining 2 egg whites until stiff.
9. Fold the cooled pudding mixture into the egg whites, until completely blended.
10. Pour pudding into a serving dish, cover, and refrigerate at least one hour before serving.
11. Stir pudding before serving.
12. This can also be used as a filling for crepes.

Nutritional information   per 1/2 cup serving, 114 calories, 1 bread and 1 fruit exchange.

Vermicelli Dessert

Saffron and pistachio nuts give this noodle pudding an exotic eastern flavor. This rich and impressive company dessert can be served warm or cold.

Preparation time 1 hour (prepare 2 cups Sweet Milk the day before)
Yield 8 servings

Ingredients
1/4 tsp. saffron
1/2 T. water
about 1/4 pound vermicelli pasta
2 1/2 T. light oil (sunflower or safflower)
2 cups Sweet Milk (see page 28)
1/4 tsp. cinnamon
1/2 cup skim milk
1/2 cup raisins
1/8 cup (21) salted pistachio nuts, natural color
1/8 cup chopped almonds

1. Soak saffron in 1/2 T. water and set aside for later use.
2. To break pasta, put in a paper bag and pound on the bag. Pieces should be about one inch long and equal 1 1/4 cups.
3. In a large skillet over medium heat, warm 2 1/2 T. oil.
4. Cook vermicelli in oil 5-7 minutes or until lightly browned, stirring occasionally.
5. Reduce heat to moderate low and add 2 cups Sweet Milk and cinnamon. Cook 15 minutes, stirring occasionally.
6. Add skim milk, saffron in water, raisins and nuts. Cook over low heat 15 minutes longer, stirring frequently.
7. Spoon into pretty serving dishes. (A raisin in the center makes a nice garnish.) Serve warm or cold.
8. Refrigerate any unused portions, covered. Freezing is not recommended.

Nutritional information per serving, 153 calories, 1 bread and 1/2 milk (whole milk) exchange.

Gelatin Desserts

1. Use 1 tablespoon unflavored gelatin.
2. Combine gelatin with 2 cups warm, unsweetened fruit juice, any kind you like.
3. Stir until gelatin dissolves.
4. Chill to the consistency of egg whites.
5. Fold in 1 cup of any fruit you like.
6. Pour into serving bowl or cups until set.

Nutritional information   will vary depending on your selection. Generally 1/3 to 1/2 cup of juice based gelatin with fruit folded in is equal to 1 fruit exchange or about 40 calories.

Strawberry Banana Dessert

Preparation time   30 minutes to prepare, 2 hours to chill
Yield   1 quart or 8 servings

Ingredients

1/2 cup water
1 T. unflavored gelatin
1 T. lemon juice
10 ounces strawberries, frozen without sugar
2 small (7 3/4-inch) very ripe bananas
1 cup Nonfat Yogurt (see page 29)
  or commercial plain nonfat yogurt
mint sprigs, garnish

1. In a saucepan heat water to boiling.
2. Meanwhile in a medium bowl soften gelatin in lemon juice. When water is boiling, add it, a little at a time, to the softened gelatin, stirring while you add it. Stir until gelatin has completely dissolved.
3. Stir frozen strawberries into hot gelatin, mashing gently.
4. Allow strawberry-gelatin mixture to cool to room temperature.
5. In a large bowl, mash the very ripe bananas, then add the strawberry gelatin. Beat well.
6. Fold in 1 cup Nonfat Yogurt (see page 29) and pour the mixture into 8 individual serving dishes or a 1 quart bowl or mold. Chill 2 hours or overnight.
7. Garnish with mint sprigs before serving.

Nutritional information   per 1/2 cup serving, 40 calories, 1 fruit exchange.

Strawberry Clouds

Preparation time 20 minutes to prepare, 2 hours to chill
Yield 3 cups, serves 6

Ingredients

1/2 cup sliced frozen strawberries
3 large eggs
1 T. unflavored gelatin
1/4 cup cold water
3 cups fresh or partially thawed sliced strawberries

1. Measure out 1/2 cup frozen sliced strawberries and set them aside. If they're whole strawberries, slice enough to equal 1/2 cup.
2. Fill a small saucepan with water (enough to cover eggs) and bring it to a boil.
3. While waiting for water to boil, run eggs under warm water, then using a heatproof strainer or tongs, dip each egg into boiling water for 30 seconds, *no longer.* Dry eggs.
4. Separate eggs, putting whites in a large mixing bowl and yolks in a small bowl.
5. Beat egg whites until stiff peaks form and set aside.
6. Beat egg yolks until well combined and lemony, set aside.
7. In a small saucepan, soften 1 T. unflavored gelatin in 1/4 cup cold water.
8. Heat the softened gelatin, stirring until crystals completely dissolve.
9. Remove pan from heat and add the 1/2 cup sliced frozen strawberries, stirring until mixture is pink and gelatin just begins to thicken, then quickly beat gelatin into egg yolks.
10. Add the yolk/gelatin mixture to the stiff egg whites, beat on high speed until thoroughly combined.
11. Pour the clouds into a serving bowl and refrigerate at least two hours.
12. To serve: Spoon 1/2 cup fresh or partially thawed strawberries over 1/2 cup clouds.

Variations Substitute peaches, cherries, blueberries or raspberries for strawberries.

Nutritional information per 1/2 cup clouds with 1/2 cup strawberries, 73 calories, 1/2 meat (medium fat), 1 fruit exchange.

Golden Waldorf

This classic fruit and nut combination, molded in apple gelatin and served with a tart blue cheese dressing is the perfect ending to a soup or sandwich meal.

Preparation time	2 hours
Yield	3 cups, serves 6

Ingredients

Gelatin

1 1/2 cups unsweetened apple juice
1 T. unflavored gelatin
1 T. lemon juice
1/2 cup cubed apple
1/2 cup diced celery
1/4 cup chopped golden raisins
1/8 cup coarsely chopped walnuts

Dressing

1/4 cup (1 ounce) crumbled Blue Cheese
1/4 cup Nonfat Yogurt (see page 29)
  or commercial plain nonfat yogurt

1. In a saucepan heat apple juice to boiling.
2. Meanwhile, in a small bowl, soften gelatin in lemon juice.
3. Slowly add boiling juice to softened gelatin, stirring all the while to dissolve.
4. When gelatin is completely dissolved, refrigerate it for 60-75 minutes or until of egg white consistency.
5. Meanwhile prepare celery, walnuts and raisins for the gelatin.
6. When gelatin has thickened, chop apple (if you chop the apple earlier, it will turn brown) and add it and the other ingredients to the gelatin, folding them in until well blended.
7. If you wish to mold the gelatin, rinse a 3 cup mold with cold water, then fill with the waldorf gelatin.
8. Refrigerate gelatin until set.
9. Unmold gelatin by immersing mold to the rim in lukewarm water for ten seconds. Fill the sink or a large bowl with lukewarm water, hold mold immersed to the rim while you count to ten. Invert on a serving plate and tap sides until you hear it "schlumpt" onto the plate.
10. Refrigerate until serving time.
11. To prepare Blue Cheese Dressing: In a small bowl stir together yogurt and blue cheese.
12. Spoon Blue Cheese Dressing around or over gelatin.

Nutritional information

per 1/2 cup serving with dressing, 95 calories, 1 1/4 fruit, 1/4 (lowfat) milk exchange
per 1/2 cup serving without dressing, 75 calories, 1 1/2 fruit, 1/7 meat (high fat) exchange

Yogurt Ideas

Take 1 cup of plain nonfat yogurt.

1. Serve flavored with 1/2 teaspoon vanilla or almond extract.
2. Flavor with 1/4 teaspoon cinnamon and 1/2 teaspoon vanilla extract.
3. Sprinkle with 1/2 cup granola and 1 T. raisins.
4. Combine with 7 finely chopped almonds, flavor with almond extract (1/4 teaspoon). Alternate with 2 cups fresh strawberries in 4 parfait glasses. Garnish with mint sprigs.
5. Combine with 1/2 cup canned crushed pineapple, well drained, and garnish with toasted coconut.
6. Combine with 1 small banana in blender. Flavor with 1/4 teaspoon almond extract and garnish with 5 chopped roasted almonds.
7. Layer banana yogurt (above, no. 6) and pineapple yogurt (above, no. 5) in dessert glasses.
8. Combine cinnamon yogurt (no. 2) with 1/2 cup applesauce.

Peanut Butter Pudding

It is good to focus on the simple things that give pleasure. My friend, Dale, expresses appreciation in the simple things. He is especially fond of perfect bananas so, while preparing this pudding, Dale comes to mind not only because of the perfect banana it contains, but because it is such a simple pleasure to make and eat.

Preparation time 10 minutes to prepare, 45 minutes to chill
Yield serves 3 (1/2 cup servings) or 1 1/2 cups

Ingredients
1 small (7 3/4-inch) perfect, ripe banana
1/2 cup Nonfat Yogurt (see page 29)
   or commercial plain nonfat yogurt
1/2 cup peanut butter, natural style
1/4 tsp. vanilla
pinch salt, optional

1. Combine all ingredients in a blender. Process on low then high speed until smooth.
2. Pour into four individual serving dishes and refrigerate.
3. Serve Cold.

Nutritional information 290 calories per serving, 2 meat exchanges (high fat), 1 1/2 fruit exchanges, 1/2 fat exchange

Independence Parfait

Preparation time	20 minutes
Yield	serves 4

Ingredients

2 cups Nonfat Yogurt (see page 29)
  or commercial plain nonfat yogurt
8 almonds
1 tsp. vanilla extract
1 cup fresh blueberries
1 cup fresh strawberries
4 strawberries, garnish

1. Combine yogurt, almonds and extract.
2. Spoon 1/4 cup blueberries into each of four parfait glasses. Top with 1/4 cup of the yogurt mixture.
3. Spoon 1/4 cup strawberries on top of yogurt layer, then finish with remaining yogurt over strawberries.
4. Garnish with a strawberry.
5. Serve immediately or chill until serving time.

Nutritional information   per serving, 88 calories or 1/2 milk (lowfat), 1 fruit exchange

CHAPTER TEN
Beverages

A Smoothie is a thick, fruity beverage that makes a delicious and refreshing summer time treat or a pleasurable accompaniment to a sandwich or salad. The naturally bright colors of these beverages reflect the fruits from which they're made. Serve them in clear glass, garnished with a berry or mint sprig.

The directions are always the same. Blend at high speed until smooth.

Verry Berry Smoothie

Preparation time	10 minutes
Yield	serves 2

Ingredients
1/4 cup sliced strawberries, fresh or frozen without sugar
1/4 cup red raspberries, fresh or frozen without sugar
1/4 cup blueberries, fresh or frozen without sugar
1/4 cup skim milk
1/2 cup unsweetened apple juice

Nutritional information per 3/4 cup serving, 68 calories, 1/8 (nonfat) milk exchange, 1 1/3 fruit exchange

Strawberry Patch Smoothie

Preparation time	10 minutes
Yield	serves 2

Ingredients
3/4 cup unsweetened apple juice
1/2 cup sliced peaches, fresh or frozen without sugar
1/2 cup sliced strawberries, fresh or frozen without sugar
1/4 cup Nonfat Yogurt (see page 29)
  or commercial nonfat yogurt

Nutritional information per 7/8 cup serving, 84 calories, 2 fruit exchanges

Banana Strawberry Smoothie

Preparation time	10 minutes
Yield	serves 2

Ingredients

1 cup sliced strawberries, fresh or frozen without sugar
1 small (7 3/4-inch) ripe banana
1/4 cup skim milk
1/4 cup Nonfat Yogurt (see page 29)
    or commercial nonfat yogurt

Nutritional information   per 7/8 cup serving, 89 calories, 1/3 milk (nonfat), 1 1/2 fruit exchange

Peach Smoothie

Preparation time	10 minutes
Yield	serves 3

Ingredients

2 cups sliced peaches, fresh or frozen without sugar
1 cup unsweetened apple juice
1 cup Nonfat Yogurt (see page 29)
    or commercial nonfat yogurt
1/4 tsp. cinnamon

Nutritional information   per 1 cup serving, 109 calories, 1/2 milk (nonfat), 1 3/4 fruit exchange

Blueberry Smoothie

Preparation time	10 minutes
Yield	serves 2

Ingredients

1 cup fresh or frozen blueberries without sugar
1/2 cup unsweetened apple juice
1/2 cup Nonfat Yogurt (see page 29)
    or commercial nonfat yogurt

Nutritional information   per 7/8 cup serving, 94 calories, 1/3 milk (nonfat), 1 3/4 fruit exchange

Banana-Pineapple Smoothie

Preparation time	10 minutes
Yield	serves 3

Ingredients

2 small (7 3/4-inch) ripe bananas
1 8-ounce can crushed pineapple, juice packed
1 cup Nonfat Yogurt (see page 29)
   or commercial nonfat yogurt

Nutritional information   per 7/8 cup serving, 127 calories, 3/4 milk (nonfat), 1 3/4 fruit exchange

Pink Satin Smoothie

Preparation time	10 minutes
Yield	1 cup, serves 1

Ingredients

1/4 cup unsweetened orange juice
1 small (7 3/4-inch) ripe banana
1/4 cup sliced strawberries, fresh or frozen, without sugar
1/4 cup Nonfat Yogurt (see page 29)
   or commercial plain nonfat yogurt

Nutritional information   per 1 cup serving, 144 calories, 1/2 milk (nonfat), 2 1/2 fruit exchanges

Rainbow Smoothie

Preparation time	10 minutes
Yield	2 cups, serves 2

Ingredients

1 small (7 3/4-inch) ripe banana
1/2 cup crushed pineapple and juice (juice packed)
1/2 cup sliced strawberries, fresh or frozen without sugar
1/2 cup Nonfat Yogurt (see page 29)
   or commercial plain nonfat yogurt

Nutritional information   per 1 cup serving, 144 calories, 3 fruit, 1/3 (nonfat) milk exchange

Banana Shake

Preparation time allow 2 hours to freeze the fruit, 3 minutes to prepare shake
Yield 2 thick, yummy shakes (3/4 cup each)

Ingredients
1 small (7 3/4-inch) very ripe banana
1 cup skim milk
1/4 tsp. vanilla
pinch nutmeg

1. Peel banana, wrap it in foil or plastic wrap and freeze 2 hours or until hard.
2. Chill two glasses (glass mugs are nice).
3. In blender briefly process frozen banana, milk and vanilla.
4. Pour into chilled glasses and garnish with nutmeg.
5. Serve immediately.

Variations *Peach Shake:* Use 1 cup sliced frozen (without sugar) peaches in place of banana. Eliminate nutmeg.
Berry Shake: Use 1 cup frozen strawberries, blueberries or raspberr raspberries in place of banana. Eliminate nutmeg.

Nutritional information (Banana Shake) per serving, 85 calories, 1/2 milk (nonfat), 1 fruit exchange
(Peach Shake) per serving, 73 calories, 1/2 milk (nonfat), 3/4 fruit exchange
(Berry Shake) per serving, about 85 calories, 1/2 milk (nonfat), 1 fruit exchange

Pineapple Cocktail

Preparation time   prepare and serve immediately
Yield   1 cup, serves 1

Ingredients

1/3 cup unsweetened pineapple juice
2/3 cup carbonated mineral water
1 slice pineapple
mint sprig, garnish

1. Pour pineapple juice into a stemmed glass, add mineral water, stirring.
2. Cut through one edge of the pineapple slice and set it over the lip of the glass, pull the mint sprig through the pineapple center.
3. Serve immediately.

Nutritional information   per serving, 45 calories, 1 fruit exchange

Eggnog

Preparation time   5 minutes
Yield   serves 1

Ingredients

1 cup nonfat (skim) milk
1 medium egg
1/2 tsp. vanilla extract
pinch nutmeg

1. Chill the serving glass by putting it in the freezer.
2. Run scalding hot water over the egg for 1 minute or parboil it.
3. Measure milk and vanilla into the blender, add the egg and process on high speed.
4. Pour the blended mixture into the chilled glass and garnish with nutmeg.
5. Serve immediately.

Nutritional information   per serving, 152 calories, 1 milk (nonfat) exchange and 1 meat (medium fat) exchange

Index

Agar, gelling substance, 21
  in Banana Cream Pie, 110
Almond(s)
  in Apple Filling, 66
  in Apricot Bread/Rolls, 37
  in Berry Fillings, 67
  in Broiled Bananas, 94
  in Peach Spoon Out, 104
  in Raisin-Nut Muffins, 48
Apple(s)
  in Chefoo's Easy Apple Puffs, 68
  in Cranberry-Raisin Pie, 113
  in Raisin Bread Pudding, 118
  in Golden Waldorf, 130
Apple Butter, recipe for, 24
  in Apple Filling, 66
  in Matzo Kugel, 122
Apple Butter Bars, 69
Apple Butter-Peanut Butter Cookies, 71
Apple-Cheese Empanados, 77
Apple Cookie Filling, 66
Apple Crumble, 96
Apple Juice
  in Golden Waldorf, 130
  in Smoothies, 133-134
Apple Kuchen, 96
Apple/Pear Tea Cake, 36
Apple Pie Filling, 108
Apple Plump, 100
Apple-Raisin Kuchen, 97
Apple Struedel, 98
Apple Tapioca, 123
Applesauce, recipe for, 25
  in Blueberry Muffins, 46
  in Cherry Spice Cake, 52
  in Matzo Kugel, 122
  in Pumpkin Bars, 60
  in Pumpkin Pie Filling, 109

  in Raisin Bread Pudding, 118
  in Tut's Carob Cake, 53
Applesauce-Nut Empanados, 77
Applesauce-Raisin Cake, 50
Apricot(s)
  in California Fruit Bread, 44
Apricot Bran Muffins, 45
Apricot Bread/Rolls, 37
Apricot Butter, recipe for, 25
  in Apricot Filling, 91
  in Glazed Pears, 95
Apricot Cheesecake, 51
Apricot Coconut Filling, 66
Apricot Pecan Confections, 85
Apricot Tea Cake, 36

Baked Apples, 94
Banana(s)
  in Broiled Bananas, 94
  in California Fruit Bread, 44
  Equivalents, 20
  in Frosty Fruit Shortcake, 58
  in Peanut Butter Pudding, 131
  in Rainbow Smoothie, 135
  Ripeness, 19
Banana Bread, 41
Banana Cream Pie, 110
Banana Drops, 72
Banana-Pineapple Smoothie, 135
Banana Pudding, 125
Banana Shake, 136
Banana Strawberry Smoothie, 134
Barbara's Stars, 64
Basic Pie Crust, 105, 108-109, 111, 113, 115
Berry-Peach-Cherry Empanados, 77
Berry Pie Filling, 108

Berry Tea Cake, 36
Beverages, 133-137
Blended Butter, recipe for, 26
    in Apple Struedel, 98
    in Peach Spoon Out, 104
    in Plum Pudding, 120
Blueberry(ies)
    in Berry Filling, 92
    in Glazed Berry Pie, 111
    in Independence Parfait, 132
    in Verry Berry Smoothie, 133
Blueberry and Rice Pudding, 125
Blueberry Clouds, 129
Blueberry Crumpet, 61
Blueberry Muffins, 46
Blueberry-Peach Kuchen, 102
Blueberry Shake, 136
Blueberry Shortcake, 59
Blueberry Smoothie, 134
Bran
    in Apricot Muffins, 45
Bread
    Apricot, 37
    Banana, 41
    Brown, 42
    California Fruit, 44
    Prune and Cheese, 40
    Raisin, 33
    Whole Wheat, 31
    Zucchini, 43
Broiled Bananas, 94
Brown Bread, 42
Butter
    Blended, 26
Brown Sugar, 11

Cake
    Applesauce-Raisin, 50
    Apricot Cheese, 51
    Carrot, 54
    Cherry Spice, 52
    Grandma's Fruit, 55
    Tea, 34-35
    Tut's Carob, 53
California Fruit Bread, 44
Caloric Values, 16-18
Cantaloupe, 93
Carbohydrates, 11-12
Carob, description of, 20
    in Peanut Butter Balls, 85
    in Tut's Carob-Cake, 53
Carob Cookies, 73
Carob Ice Milk, 124
Carob Pie, 124
Carob Pudding, 124
Carob-Raisin Filling, 91
Carrot Cake, 54
Cashew Halvah, 74

Cheese, description of, 20
    in Prune and Cheese Bread, 40
    in Applesauce-Cheddar Filling, 90
    in Apricot Cheesecake, 51
Cheese-Fruit Tea Cake, 36
Cheese-Raisin Empanados, 77
Cheesecake, Apricot, 51
Chefoo's Easy Apple Puffs, 68
Cherry(ies)
    in Glazed Berry Pie, 111
Cherry Clouds, 129
Cherry Custard Pie, 112
Cherry (Cookie) Filling, 67
Cherry Spice Cake, 52
Cherry Struedel, 99
Cinnamon Yogurt, 131
Coconut
    in Apricot Cheesecake, 51
    in Apricot Coconut Filling, 66
    in Filled Oat Bars, 76
    in Orange Chiffon Pie, 114
    in Peanut Butter Carob Balls, 85
    in Pineapple Filling, 67
Coconut Bars, 75
Coconut Pie Shell, 106, 110, 114, 116
Cookie(s)
    Apple Butter Bars, 69
    Apple Butter-Peanut Butter, 71
    Apricot Pecan Confections, 85
    Banana Drops, 72
    Carob, 73
    Cashew Halvah, 74
    Chefoo's Easy Apple Puffs, 68
    Coconut Bars, 75
    Date Peanut Clusters, 84
    Empanados, 77
    Filled Oat Bars, 76
    Gingerbread People, 80
    Jackie's Roll-ups, 65
    Janet's Best Date, 78
    Kiflis, 64
    Peanut Butter Balls, 86
    Peanut Butter Carob Balls, 85
    Pinwheels, 65
    Raisin Drops, 83
    Sandwich, 65
    Sticks and Stones, 79
Cookie Fillings,
    Apple, 66
    Apricot Coconut, 66
    Cherry, 67
    Fig, 65
    Peach/Berry, 67
    Peanut Butter Raisin, 67
    Pineapple, 67
    Prune, 66
Corn Kernels, 126
Corn Syrup, 11, 12

Cottage Cheese
  as dip, 93
  in Almond Filling, 90
  in Carob-Raisin Filling, 91
  in Raisin Kugel, 121
Cottage Cheese Tea Cake, 36
Cranberry-Raisin Pie, 113
Cream, 17
Cream Cheese, 12
Custard, 117
Crepes, 87-92
Crepe Fillings
  Almond, 90
  Applesauce-Cheddar, 90
  Apricot, 91
  Banana, 131
  Berry, 92
  Carob-Raisin, 91
  Pumpkin, 109
  Sandcastle, 126
Currants
  in Cashew Halvah, 74

Date(s)
  in Banana Drops, 72
  in Broiled Bananas, 94
  in Brown Bread, 42
  in Carob Cookies, 73
  in Carob Pudding, 124
  in Cherry Spice Cake, 52
  in Filled Oat Bars, 76
  in Filled Rolls, 38
  in Gingerbread People, 80
  in Granola, 70
  in Granola Bars, 82
  in Janet's Best Date Cookies, 78
  in Old Fashioned Bread Pudding, 119
  in Plum Pudding, 120
  in Raisin Drops, 83
  in Sandcastle Pudding, 126
  in Sticks and Stones, 79
  in Tut's Carob Cake, 53
  in Whole Wheat Bread, 31
Date-Peanut Clusters, 84
Dessert Cheeses, 20
Dextrose, 11
Diabetes, 9, 10, 12, 13
Dried Fruits
  in Tea Cake, 36

Eggnog, 137
Empanados, 77
Envelopes, 64
Exchange System, 14-18

Fats, description of, 12
Feast on a Diabetic Diet, 13
Fiber, 10-12
Fig Filling, 65
Filled Oat Bars, 76
Filled Rolls, 38
Flours, 17, 21
Food Exchanges, 14-18
Food Groups, 14
Frosty Fruit Shortcake, 58
Fructose, 11, 12
Fruit(s), 17, 93-104
  Serving ideas, 93
Fruit Cake, Grandma's, 55
Fruit Cocktail, 93
Fruit Salad, 93
Fruit Shortcakes, 58-59

Gelatin, 21
Gelatin Desserts, 128-130
Gingerbread, 56
Gingerbread People, 80
Glazed Berry Pie, 111
Glazed Pears, 95
Golden Waldorf, 130
Grains, 21
Grandma's Fruit Cake, 55
Granola, 70
Granola Bars, 82

Hippopotamus Pie, 116
Hippopotamus Pudding, 116
Honey, 10, 11
Honeydew Melon, 93

Icing, 49
  see also: Yogurt Cheese Icing, 30
Independence Parfait, 132
Ingredients, description of, 19
Insulin, 12
Invert Sugar, 11

Jackie's Roll-ups, 65
Janet's Best Date Cookies, 78

Kiflis, 64
Kuchen
  Apple, 96
  Apple-Raisin, 97
  Pear, 97

Laurel's Kitchen, 13
Lecithin/Oil, 27
Legumes, 11

Mandarin Tapioca Pudding, 123
Maple Syrup, 11
    in Raisin Maple Syrup, 28
Meal Planning, 13-18
Melba Kuchen, 103
Matzo Kugel, 122
Milk, 17, 22, 28
    Nonfat, 12
Minerals, 11
Molasses, 10, 11
Muffin(s)
    Apricot Bran, 45
    Baking Tips, 45
    Blueberry, 46
    Orange, 47
    Raisin-Nut, 48

Nonfat Milk, 12
Nonfat Yogurt, 12, 29
Nut Tea Cake, 36
Nutrition, 11-17
The Nutrition Almanac, 13
Nuts, 16

Oats, 21
Old Fashioned Bread Pudding, 119
Orange(s)
    in Mandarin Tapioca, 123
    in Spiced Fruit, 95
Orange Chiffon Pie, 114
Orange Juice
    in Apricot Cheesecake, 51
    in Glazed Pears, 95
    in Orange Chiffon Pie, 114
    in Peanut Butter Raisin Filling, 67
    in Pink Satin Smoothie, 135
    in Spiced Fruit, 95
    in Sunshine Squares, 57
Orange Muffins, 47
Orange Rind
    in Sunshine Squares, 57

Peach(es)
    in Blueberry-Peach Kuchen, 102
    in Chefoo's Easy Peach Puffs, 69
    in Spiced Fruit, 95
    in Strawberry Patch Smoothie, 133
    in Tangy Peach Pie, 115
    in Tangy Peach Pudding, 115
Peach Clouds, 129
Peach Crisp, 101

Peach Custard Pie, 112
Peach (Cookie) Filling, 67
Peach (Tea Cake) Filling, 36
Peach Kuchen, 102
Peach/Pear Struedel, 99
Peach Pie Filling, 108
Peach Shake, 136
Peach Shortcake, 59
Peach Smoothie, 134
Peach Spoon Out, 104
Peanut Butter
    as dip, 93
    in Apple Butter Cookies, 71
    in Date Peanut Clusters, 84
Peanut Butter Balls, 86
Peanut Butter Carob Balls, 85
Peanut Butter Pudding, 131
Peanut Butter Raisin (Cookie) Filling, 67
Pear(s)
    in Apple Tea Cake, 36
    in Glazed Pears, 95
    in Spiced Fruit, 95
Pear (Pie) Filling, 108
Pear Kuchen, 97
Pecan(s)
    in Apricot Pecan Confections, 85
    in Apricot Bread/Rolls, 37
    in Pineapple Filling, 67
Pie(s), 105-116
    crust, 105
    shells, 105-107
Pineapple
    in Banana-Pineapple Smoothie, 135
    in California Fruit Bread, 44
    in Carrot Cake, 54
    in Coconut Bars, 75
    in Filled Oat Bars, 76
    in Frosty Fruit Shortcake, 58
    in Glazed Berry Pie, 111
    in Hippopotamus Pie, 116
    in Orange Chiffon Pie, 116
    in Rainbow Smoothie, 135
    in Zucchini Bread, 43
Pineapple Cocktail, 137
Pineapple Empanados, 77
Pineapple (Cookie) Filling, 67
Pineapple Plumps, 100
Pineapple Tea Cake, 36
Pink Satin Smoothie, 135
Pinwheels, 65
Plum Pudding, 120
Poppy Seed Tea Cake, 36
Protein, 12, 13
Prunes
    in Filled Rolls, 38-39
    in Plum Pudding, 120
Prune and Cheese Bread, 40
Prune (Cookie) Filling, 66
Puddings, 117-132

Puff Pancake Dessert, 62
Pumpkin Bars, 60
Pumpkin (Pie) Filling, 109

Quick Apricot Butter, 25

Rainbow Smoothie, 135
Raisin(s)
    in Apple Butter-Peanut Butter
        Cookies, 71
    in Apple Pie Filling, 108
    in Applesauce-Raisin Cake, 50
    in Banana Bread, 41
    in California Fruit Bread, 44
    in Carob-Raisin Filling, 91
    in Carrot Cake, 54
    in Cashew Halvah, 74
    in Chefoo's Easy Apple Puffs, 68
    in Golden Waldorf, 130
    in Grandma's Fruit Cake, 55
    in Granola, 70
    for illustrating, 81
    in Old Fashioned Bread Pudding, 119
    in Peach Kuchen, 102
    in Peanut Butter Balls, 86
    in Peanut Butter Carob Balls, 85
    in Plum Pudding, 120
    in Pumpkin Bars, 60
    in Vermicelli Dessert, 127
Raisin Bread, 33
Raisin Bread Pudding, 118
Raisin Drops, 83
Raisin Kugel, 121
Raisin Maple Syrup, 28
Raisin-Nut Muffins, 48
Raspberry(ies)
    in Berry Filling, 92
    in Glazed Berry Pie, 111
    in Melba Kuchen, 102
    in Verry Berry Smoothie, 133
Raspberry Clouds, 129
Raspberry Shake, 136
Rice, 21
Rice Puddings, 125

Sandcastle Pudding, 126
Sandwich Cookies, 65
Seeds, 16
Shakes, 136
Shortcake(s)
    Blueberry, 59
    Frosty Fruit, 58
    Peach, 59
    Strawberry, 59
Smith, Lendon H., M.D., 10
Smoothies, 133-135

Soy Flour, 21
Spiced Fruit, 95
Spices, 22
Sticks and Stones, 79
Storage, 19
Strawberry(ies)
    in Berry Filling, 92
    in Frosty Fruit Shortcake, 58
    in Glazed Berry Pie, 111
    in Independence Parfait, 132
    in Smoothies, 133-134
Strawberry Banana Dessert, 128
Strawberry Clouds, 129
Strawberry Custard Pie, 112
Strawberry Patch Smoothie, 133
Strawberry Pineapple Pie, 111
Strawberry Shake, 136
Strawberry Shortcake, 59
Sugar, 9-12
Sunshine Squares, 57
Sweet Milk, description of, 28
    in Apple Kuchen, 102
    in Applesauce-Raisin Cake, 50
    in Blueberry Crumpet, 61
    in Cherry Custard Pie, 112
    in Cherry Spice Cake, 52
    in Custard, 117
    in Gingerbread, 56
    in Old Fashioned Bread Pudding, 119
    in Peach Kuchen, 102
    in Pumpkin Pie Filling, 109
    in Raisin Bread Pudding, 118
    in Raisin Drops, 83
    in Raisin-Nut Muffins, 48
    in Rice Pudding, 126
    in Vermicelli Dessert, 127
Sweet Rolls, 35
Sweet Spices, 22
Sweeteners, Artificial, 10

Tangy Peach Pie, 115
Tangy Peach Pudding, 115
Tapioca
    in Apple Tapioca, 123
    in Mandarin Tapioca, 123
Tea Cakes
    Number 1, 34
    Number 2, 34
    Number 3, 35
Triticale flakes, 21, 70
Tut's Carob Cake, 53

Vegetables, 15
    canned, 12
Vermicelli Dessert, 127
Verry Berry Smoothie, 133
Vitamins, 11, 12

Walnut(s)
    in Apple Pie Filling, 108
    in Apple Struedel, 98
    in Apricot Bread/Rolls, 37
    in Banana Bread, 41
    in Carob Cookies, 73
    in Fig Filling, 65
    in Matzo Kugel, 122
    in Plum Pudding, 120
    in Prune Filling, 66
    in Pumpkin Bars, 60
    in Zucchini Bread, 43
Wheat Germ Crust, 107, 112
Whole Wheat Bread, 31
Whole Wheat Bread Pudding, 118
Whole Wheat Crepes, 89
Whole Wheat Crust, 107

Yeasted Breads, 31-33
Yogurt
    in Banana Cream Pie, 110
    Cheese, 12, 30
    Cheese Icing, 30
    Crepes, 88
    in Frosty Fruit Shortcake, 58
    in Hippopotamus Pie, 116
    in Independence Parfait, 132
    in Kiflis, 64
    Nonfat, 29, 51
    in Peach Kuchen, 102
    Serving Ideas, 93, 131-132
    in Smoothies, 134-135

Zucchini Bread, 43